REDON

Phidal

"You ruffle the plumage of dreams and night in the midst of our silence."

Stéphane Mallarmé

Odilon Redon only just missed being born at sea. In the middle of April 1840, when our story begins, his parents were sailing across the Atlantic on their journey from New Orleans to Bordeaux. Bertrand Redon had left his native Bordeaux ten years earlier to seek his fortune in America and was now returning home as planned, bringing with him a tidy fortune, his wife (who was the daughter of French colonists and whom he had met in Louisiana) and their little five-year-old son. On April 20th, 1840, one week after the family had reached France, their second son Odilon was born. His health was so poor, however, that his parents soon decided to send him to breathe the fresher air of the countryside. There were no problems about where to send him since the family owned a small estate at Peyrelebade, in the district of Médoc, a strip of land lying between the ocean and the province of Gironde, "a place of water and air", as Redon was to call it later. When Odilon, still a baby, was taken there by coach, his father's isolated stretch of land was still growing wild.

The child, however, had a comfortable life: he was brought up by a nurse, in the care of a friendly uncle who also looked after the estate, and his parents frequently came to visit him. Above all he was free: "My greatest fortune was that the doctors said that too much studying would be bad for me," he wrote later in the diary he kept throughout his life and through which we can try to understand the secrets which his paintings hint at, but never fully reveal.

Odilon grew into a quiet, shy boy, who was still practically illiterate at the age of eleven, though he had already won prizes for his painting and was an expert in the art of daydreaming. He was not one of those children who race across the open fields looking for animals to chase; he preferred to sit and meditate. He preferred the adventures of the mind to physical effort. He could often be found sitting in a quiet, shady corner of the garden where he had settled down for the day. He would sit and watch the blades of grass blowing in the wind or sit and stare at a pebble. He was already a keen observer of nature. People interested him, too, but he was shy and the solitary life he led at Peyrelebade accentuated his shyness even further. In any case, the inhabitants of Médoc were not very talkative people. They had uncommunicative faces which Odilon could never manage to understand; they were silent people standing in the mist rising from the heath. They left a deep impression on the young boy, and were to reappear as mysterious characters in his drawings. Redon felt more at home with nature. One of his favourite pastimes was watching the clouds go by. He would lie stretched out on the ground for hours, sometimes for a whole day, in lonely spots in the countryside. The clouds in the Médoc sky were very beautiful. Blown by the wind from the ocean, they continually changed their shape, and Odilon's imagination knew no bounds. He saw objects and characters in the clouds that no-one else could have seen. It was his father who had taught him to play with the clouds. His father-an explorer, an adventurer, a strong man who, in Louisiana, had been in charge of the work of many other men. Tough and yet capable of tenderness. Odilon admired him greatly.

The time came when he had to go back to his mother and his brother. After his eleventh birthday he left for Bordeaux where school awaited him. Peyrelebade, however, remained part of his life for many years, since he returned there every summer to continue his dreams.

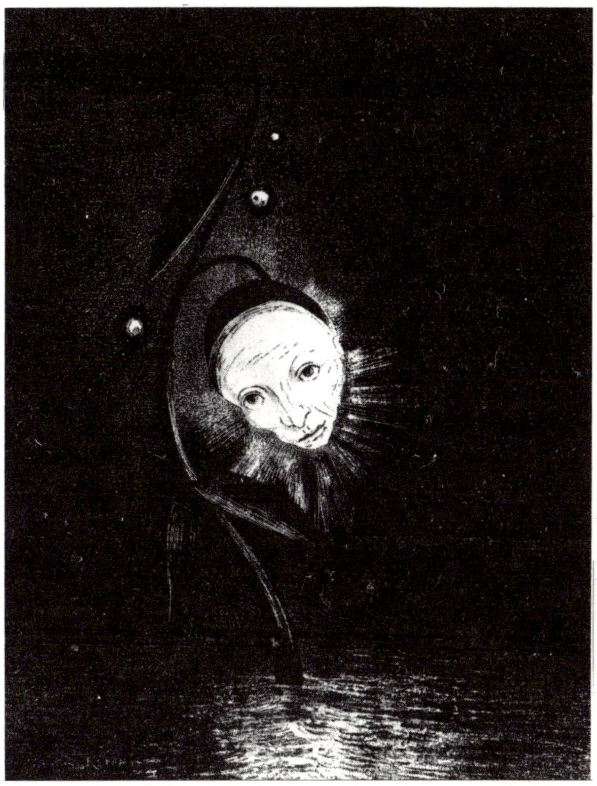

The Marsh Flower, a Sad, Human Face
Bibliothèque Nationale, Cabinet des Estampes, Paris.

He appears not to have been particularly interested in his schoolwork in Bordeaux, whereas it was with great enthusiasm that he went to study drawing with the artist Stanislas Gorin. An excellent relationship grew up between the master and his pupil, based on what could be called mutual independence. Gorin taught Redon technique, but he did so in a way that was never boring: he alternated exercises with the study of famous works which he analyzed in detail, and Redon listened to every word. The techniques used, the use of light and shade, the colours, the artist's intentions: Redon learnt all this and more. Together they went to exhibitions. Some of the greatest painters of the day held exhibitions in Bordeaux: Millet, Corot, Moreau, Delacroix. Gorin observed how the young man was filled with passion at the colours and forms of the paintings of Delacroix, and was delighted about it. Without pushing Redon in any particular direction (something Gorin had no intention of doing), Gorin was helping Redon form his artistic sensitivity.

When Redon was seventeen, his family decided that the time had come for him to start taking his studies seriously: he was to study architecture at the Ecole des Beaux-Arts in Paris. He went to Paris without much enthusiasm and the matter was solved when he failed the entrance exam. Plans were changed, and at the age of eighteen, Redon was accepted in the painting class of the influential Gérome. Although Redon did everything he could to adapt to the rules of academic teaching, the results were not good. Years later he remembered the tension that was created in the class whenever Gérome approached his easel: for Redon it was torture to hear all the criticism that was poured on his attempts. "He manifestly sought to inculcate in me his own way of seeing things and to make of me a disciple, or to make me disgusted with art itself," Redon later confessed. The image of his less famous teacher Gorin came back to him and Gorin's words rang in his ears: "Never make one stroke with the pencil until you are in full possession of your sensibility and your reason." Redon felt that this was the principle he should abide by, at any cost. After his unhappy experience with Gérome, Redon was more determined than ever to find his own style regardless of whether or not it was in line with the official teachings. This, however, was no easy task. When he was twenty he travelled to the North of Spain. He stored everything he saw in his memory: the landscape of the Pyrenees, the gloomy countryside of Biscay, the enchanting women, the sun-scorched rocks and the beaches abandoned by the sea. But at this time he neither painted nor drew them. Back in Bordeaux he chanced to make the acquaintance of an extraordinary figure, the scientist Armand Clavaud. In the isolation and peacefulness of provincial life, Clavaud was carrying out research, the theories of which were a revelation for Redon. In addition to the study of flowers – he was an expert on the flora of Gironde and possessed a remarkable collection of flowers to which he was continually adding new species – Clavaud delved into the analysis of the lower forms of animal life, convinced that there was a basic link between animal and vegetable life. "He worked with things infinitely small," wrote Redon in his diary, attracted like Clavaud by the microscope and the amazing images it revealed. "He examined the boundaries of the imperceptible world, searching for a form of life halfway between animals and plants, a flower or a being, a mysterious element that becomes an animal for a few hours under the influence of light."

Clavaud was not only a microbiologist but also a man with many different intellectual interests: he was familiar with Hindu poetry and discussed it with Redon; he was well informed about literary movements, and opened up his library to his young friend. Redon thus read Baudelaire's *Les Fleurs du mal*, dreamed about the visionary tales of Edgar Allan Poe, and discovered the recently published works of Gustave Flaubert. His artistic personality was enriched by his reading, though it was to bear fruit only later.

From 1860 to 1870 Redon tried his hand at almost everything. He wrote several interesting articles about art for a Bordeaux newspaper. He travelled to Paris several times and immersed himself in the peace and quiet of the countryside, and, between trips, in Bordeaux he played the violin during musical evenings with his brother. Remembering the sculpture lessons he had taken several years before, Redon started to model in clay. He copied the works of old masters and painted a self-portrait and some small landscapes of places he had visited (the "sweet, melancholic Brittany", for example), he made sketches and did some etchings. He learnt the technique of etching from the engraver Rodolphe Bresdin, a misunderstood artist whose fantastic compositions Redon admired: imaginary buildings, huge forests, scenes with tiny creatures in the foreground, all represented accurately and vividly. One day Bresdin said to Redon: "You see that chimney flue? What does it say to you? It tells me a whole legend. If you have the power to observe it well and understand it, you may imagine the strangest, most bizarre scene and if it is based upon and remains within the limits of this simple area of wall, your dream will be reality. Therein lies art." Redon reasoned that in Gérome's classes the chimney flue was nothing else but a chimney flue. Bresdin was subversive for his age. He also used the word "dream" which was to become the key-word to Redon's art. Redon recognized his debt to his new master by signing his first etching, entitled *The Ford* (1865), "by a pupil of Bresdin". *The Ford* was followed by other works, all drawn in black. Mountain landscapes recur, with the rocks of the Pyrenees, and figures on horseback. The drawing is always precise, as Bresdin had taught him. Redon was attracted by black, which seemed to him to convey the results of his research both as a man and a painter. In 1870 the outbreak of war put an end to Redon's uncertainties. He enlisted immediately, despite the fact that he had been declared unfit for military service. He spent one year fighting in the Loire valley and was then discharged. Although physically weaker as a result of the hardships he had faced, he emerged from the war stronger and more determined in character.

He was full of new energy. He looked again at his sketches and drawings, and found that they held new meaning for him. He finally became aware of his natural gifts. All that remained was to set to work. He moved to Paris, where he lived in a small studio in Montparnasse. On the wall he hung a reproduction of a work that he felt was in keeping with the works that he would produce: it was an engraving by Dürer entitled *Melancholy*, showing a seated woman lost in her thoughts, surrounded by a whole series of different objects which are all accurately drawn but whose meanings, probably symbolic, are not clear. Other artists from whom Redon drew inspiration were Rembrandt, the "master of shade" and Leonardo da Vinci, whom he admired for his drawings of the human figure and his skilful use of light and shade making his facial expressions incomparable. Redon felt the need to study the human body and followed courses at the Ecole de Médecine. When he visited the Natural History Museum, where he declared himself surprised by the "relative contexture of all beings," he also felt that he wished to draw the human form in his own way, as his imagination dictated, by enlarging or reducing the size of one part of it: the face, the eyes represented symbolically, isolated from the rest, fragments of reality detached from their usual context and thus mysterious.

The "monsters" seen in his lithographs were born in this way.

Redon, however, had started with etchings and charcoal drawings and moved to lithography only at a later date. "This medium," he wrote, referring to charcoal, "has no beauty in itself and thus is suited to my research into light and shade and the invisible. It is a medium that does not appeal to artists and has been neglected. With charcoal it is impossible to be amusing; you can only be serious." Technique, of course, was important, and Redon was a master of it, feeling at the time far more at ease with charcoal than with paints. "It is a medium which demands equal doses of clearsightedness and logic at the moment of inspiration." When he took up lithography in 1878 he basically did it to reproduce his charcoal drawings, to "broadcast" them, as he himself put it. By now he was sure of what he was doing; he was no longer Bresdin, nor Clavaud and he was not imitating Corot or Rembrandt: he was Redon and he was producing art in the way that he wanted.

Between 1878 and 1888 he worked very hard. For the first part of the decade, however, his work was virtually ignored by critics. His name was not known at all to the general public and art dealers and publishers would have nothing to do with his work. Why was this?

To find out, let us examine for a moment his first album of lithographs, entitled *Dans le rêve* (In the dream). It consists of ten lithographs and a frontispiece. In the first a face – drawn in a clear, realistic way – appears closed up like a cocoon or a berry; the title is *Eclosion* (Hatching Out). The second is called *Germination*: bubbles of different sizes are hovering in space, some of them very small and blurred; as they get larger they take on the appearance of a mask. In the centre there is a face. It is real, well-drawn, but it is in the middle of the sky. In the other prints the meaning is more explicit: in *Le joueur* (Three Tree Trunks with the Dice Bearer), for example, a man, standing alone in the middle of tree trunks, is carrying a huge dice on his shoulders and is staggering beneath its weight. Proportions are altered, the dice is huge and the man tiny. This is another of the aspects which make Redon's pictures symbolic. His way of giving expression to an idea is less mysterious here than in certain other works. The human face is a recurring image also in Redon's later collections. The faces have sad, composed expressions and are disturbing in the way they are placed on bowls, egg boxes or in the centre of marsh flowers, with a touch of the bizarre about them which seems to modern eyes to take away some of their dramatic power. In the album dedicated to Edgar Allan Poe, which first appeared in 1882, the bizarre was already present in the subjects he chose to illustrate and Redon merely emphasizes it with his drawings. Redon's captions, accompanying his prints, the are no less bizarre: "The eye like a marvellous balloon sets off on a journey towards the infinite"; "Before the black sun of melancholy, Lénor appeared"; "A mask tolling the hour of death" and "The angel of certitude on the horizon and in the sky a questioning look".

"I do not think that my work is appreciated much by professional lithographers," Redon admitted. "Perhaps they are right." He never defines or explains; he limits himself to making allusions and, in his own words, "opening the door to the mysterious." This, in the period of naturalism, when men were attracted by science and positive reasoning, made his work scandalous, as Redon himself was well aware. So why did he persevere? The drawings dedicated to Poe were followed by other series of lithographs – *Origines* (Origins), *La Tentation de Saint-Antoine* (The Temptation of St. Anthony), *Hommage à Goya* (Homage to Goya) and *Apocalypse* in 1899 – which were all full of disturbing scenes. As he himself said, "It is only after making an effort of willpower to represent with minute care a blade of grass, a stone, a branch, the face of an old wall, that I am overcome by the irresistible urge to create something imaginary." This he confirmed years later, when he had reached his maturity as a man and an artist. "Nature demands that we shall obey the gifts which she has given us. Mine led me into the world of dreams; I suffered the torments of imagination and the surprises which it presented to me under the pencil." And on another occasion: "Nothing in art can be done by will alone. Everything is done by docile submission to the coming of the unconscious." Odilon Redon went on producing works in black at a time when other artists were painting canvases full of sparkling colours. He worked hard and in isolation, but was not completely alone. In 1881 he married Camille Falte, originally from the Ile de Bourbon though she had lived in Paris for some time. For Camille (Redon affectionately called her "ma Parque"), he made an exception to his rule by painting a colour portrait of her in 1882. Two years previously he had painted his beloved Peyrelebade in oils: there is a tall tree trunk in the foreground and a small figure in the background. The place he knew so well had "forced" him to paint in colour. Landscapes, in fact, were something Redon never gave up painting.

With Camille's support and his own determination, convinced as he was that what he was doing was right because he was doing it with sincerity, Redon was able to put up with all the incomprehension and difficulty. He even had to face economic difficulties, something he was not accustomed to, especially since he had been born and brought up in a family that was very comfortably off. His wife fought all the battles with the art dealers and printers, leaving her husband free to give expression to his poetic inspiration.

In 1881 the first exhibition of Redon's work was held in the editorial offices of the review *La Vie Moderne*. It was a low key exhibition, even the paper itself did not take the trouble to announce it. One year later, his lithographs were exhibited in the halls of another newspaper, *Le Gaulois*, and this time certain influential critics were impressed. One was Emile Hennequin who openly praised Redon's work and introduced him to to the poet Mallarmé. The two immediately became great friends. Back in 1864 Mallarmé had written to a friend, "I invent a language which I can define in these words: painting is not so much the thing as the effect it produces." To Redon he said, "You ruffle the plumage of dreams and night in the midst of our silence." Redon, the introvert, gave his friendship to Mallarmé and a few others besides. With artists like Seurat, Signac, Cross, Angrand and Dubois-Piellet he founded the Society of Independent Artists. In 1884 the "Indépendants" held their first exhibition, and the novelist Huysmans wrote enthusiastically about Redon, emphasizing his ability as a master of "nightmare". Others, however, including the public, refused to accept him for the very same reason. Two years later Redon took part in the Impressionist Exhibition: Redon was on very good terms with the Impressionists and, like them, loved painting in the open air. Being a symbolist, however, he differed from them in that he always wanted to go beyond what he saw. Redon was about to come out of his period of isolation. His "black" works were well known in Belgium and Holland, countries where his work appeared to be better understood than in France. He was, therefore, pleased to accept the invitation to take part in the "Salon des XX" in Brussels. Between 1885 and 1886 Redon's emotional life suffered two blows: in 1885 his childhood friend Jules Boisse died and a year later he lost his son, Jean, aged just a few months. "The death of a baby leaves the heart in mourning," he wrote, "the memory is of an infinitely gentle feeling which has been destroyed and a difficult sadness remains in one's frustrated soul." During this time, Redon's fame was spreading: those who only knew him through his works and had been struck by his disturbing and sometimes terrifying images (the drawings for Flaubert's *Tentation de Saint-Antoine*, for example) thought of him as a demon, a man who frequented the devil, living in a world of nightmares. Imagine their surprise when they finally met him and found themselves face to face with an amiable, well- balanced person, fully in control of his life and his emotions. Then there were those who had no preconceived idea of the artist, but simply wanted to know the hidden meaning behind his "black" works. In his diary, Redon tells of a significant episode that took place in 1888: "A naive young Englishman came to see me one day, telling me that he had crossed the Channel to see me in order to discover the genesis of my works. 'We know the effects,' he said, 'but I would like to know more about the cause.' I learnt later from a friend in London that the young man was surprised and puzzled after his visit, because all I could give him was a smile. 'I didn't learn anything from M. Redon,' he said. The truth is that you cannot really say anything about what your hands create during the moment of artistic inspiration. It is very often a surprise to you as well: you have reached your goal and that's all. What else can you say? Why analyze it? It would be useless to do so anyway. It's better just to be happy about it and continue, leaving the rest to the critics and the philosophers."

In 1889 Mme. Redon gave birth to Ari, their second son. His intense little face appears in numerous sketches and pastel drawings. In the past Redon had always done portraits of friends, fellow artists, members of the family, and acquaintances in pencil or charcoal. From 1890 Redon's methods were to change: he began to prefer oils and pastels to the blacks he had made so much use of previously. In a letter written in 1894 to his Belgian friend, Edmond Picard, he spoke of his move in the direction of colour: "I can feel the moment coming when time is worth twice as much, the moment when the artist knows himself and stops wandering. A master of my medium, in a small domain,

I feel – more than ever before – the joy that work can give. Pastels have given me new hope of giving full expression to my dreams. The colours have a happiness that relaxes me: they are leading me to something different, something new." Again he speaks of giving expression to his dreams: his technique may change, but he is still true to his vocation. Although he started working almost exclusively in colour, his black pictures were still much admired. The Belgian publisher Jules Destrées published a catalogue of his lithographs in Brussels (1891). In Paris in the same year the Symbolists held a banquet in honour of Jean Moréas. A new artistic and literary trend was in the air, one that Redon had in many ways anticipated: the pictorial representation of symbols or thoughts in such a way as to suggest feelings rather than express them fully. When Maurice Denis exhibited his *Hommage à Cézanne* (Homage to Cézanne) in 1900, he portrayed Redon in a place of honour. A school began to form around Redon who was thus no longer professionally alone. The number of admirers and collectors of his work grew. Exhibitions were held in Paris, Brussels, La Haye, Gand, Amsterdam, Chicago, New York and Boston. Success had finally arrived. In addition to his old friends he was now viewed with affection and respect by the new generation of artists who regarded him as a master. In his house on the right bank, in the Avenue de Wagram, Redon regularly received other artists and literary figures and once a week, over a dish of Mme. Redon's famous curry, there was lively discussion of the new trends in art. Matisse came to pay homage to Redon and spoke of how he had been influenced by his new works.
Redon's transition to colour took place during the last decade of the 19th century and lasted until his death. His favourite themes were portraits, flowers, myths and religion. In his portraits, his personal approach to his subject is combined with a desire to reflect reality (an aspect that was very important for Redon). In his portrait of Ari, painted in 1886, his love for the child shows through and there is also much attention paid to the boy's personality, evidence of the respectful way Redon brought up his son from a very early age. In the portrait of Violette Heymann, done in 1909, the profusion of wild flowers facing the profile of the young girl reflects the spiritual nature of her thoughts. For Redon there is no difference between the world of nature and the soul. Both breathe and both are, therefore, alive. In the paintings devoted only to flowers, there is a vitality that makes the definition "Still Life" inappropriate. The theme of nature was dear also to his friends, the Impressionists, but in Redon's work there is something more: the technique and the colours give a sense of vibration and anxiety that goes beyond the visible reality.
The works devoted to mythology continue Redon's mysterious and visionary tradition. His fantastic "dream" images are sometimes devastatingly forceful, as in *Roger and Angelica* or *Phaeton*. What gives these pictures their dream-like impression is the remarkable use of colour, the "*sfumato*" which envelopes the whole scene like a cloud, giving horses, chariots, people and everything else the quality of a fantastic vision. Redon's particular style makes even normal things magical, such as the tree in blossom where the buds appear to be pearls. During his mature period, Redon also used to put his ability to the test by taking up new challenges. His friend Gustave Fayet, the owner of the Abbey of Fontfroide near Montpellier, asked him to take part in the restoration of the old building. This was in 1910; Redon was spending the winter in Cannes and was therefore quite close to Montpellier and Fontfroide. His specific task was to decorate the library of the abbey. Having proved his ability as an artisan by solving all the preliminary problems, Redon got ready to paint. He used a mixture of tempera, kaolin, oil and pastel which he had tried out on other occasions. His themes were the Day and the Night: light and shade, a kind of synthesis of his whole life's work. In the first panel, Night, we find the black figures of his early works, the sad, mysterious faces who never reveal the secrets they seem to be hiding. It is not an escape from reality; it is another side of reality, the side not normally seen. There are monsters: the creeping insect turning into a snake and a butterfly with the head of a man. Alongside them, however, the flowers are blossoming and Apollo's chariot lets forth its triumphal song. Redon has learnt how to overcome his anguish.
When his son Ari left for the war in 1914, Redon was concerned about his safety. After seeing him once when he came home on leave, he was left without news for a long time. He decided to travel from Bièvres where he spent most of his time (Peyrelebade had been mortgaged and then sold) to look for news of Ari in Paris.
He fell ill from the anxiety and fatigue of the journey and had to take to bed. His son came out of the war alive, but Redon never saw him again: he died on July 6th 1916.
The simple facts of Redon's public life contrast with the intense activity of his inner soul which the artist analyzed and evoked for us in his work. After all, as he himself used to say, we should all try to write the story of our own heart.

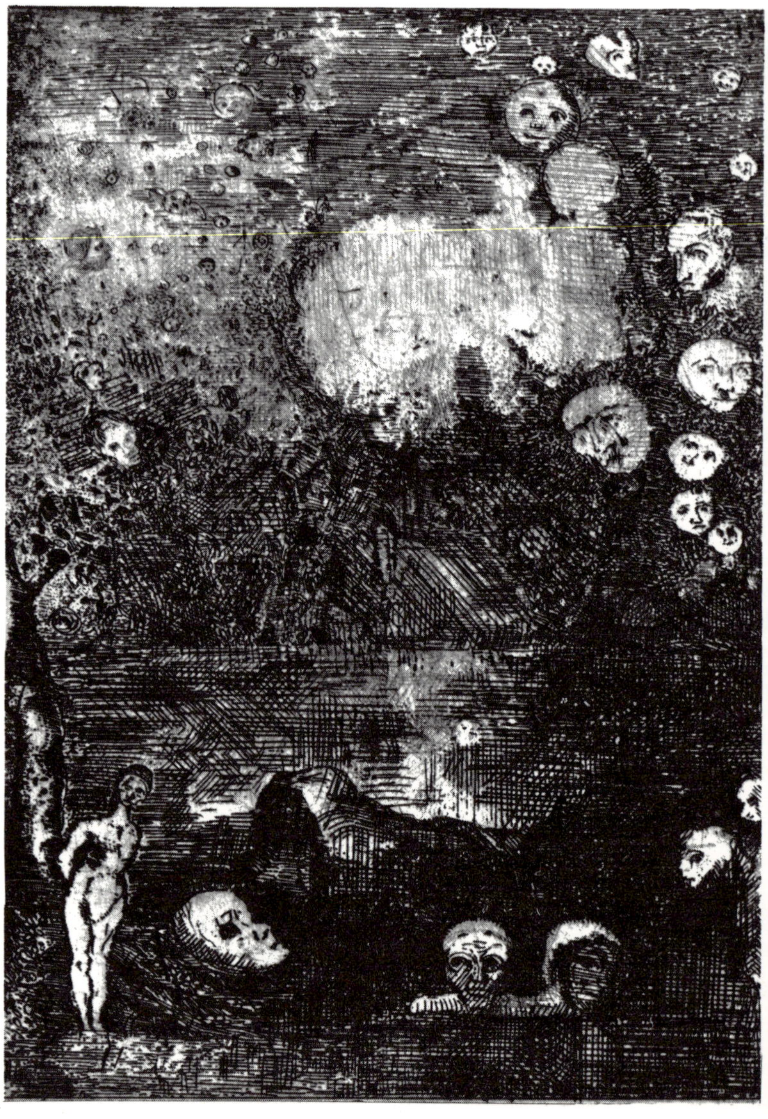

Fantastic Vision - 1880 ca. Etching, Bibliothèque Nationale, Cabinet des Estampes, Paris.

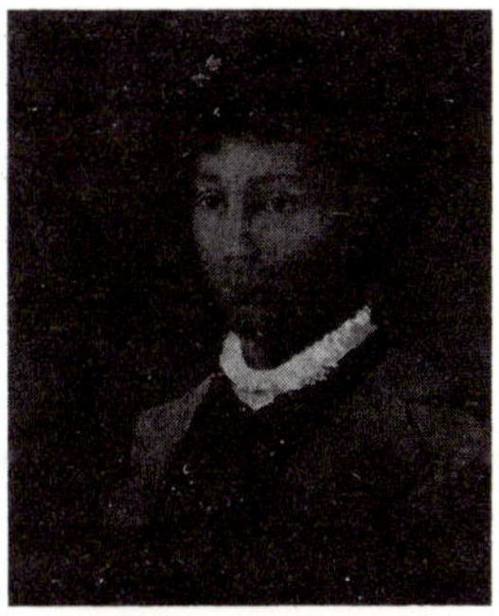

1. Madame Redon - 1882. Musée du Louvre, Paris - *This canvas portraying Camille Falte, Redon's wife, belongs to the period when the artist was principally concerned with charcoal drawings and lithography, known as "the period of black pictures". Although here he uses colour, they are all subdued tones, the only exception being the white used for the collar and the tiny daisy in his wife's hair.*

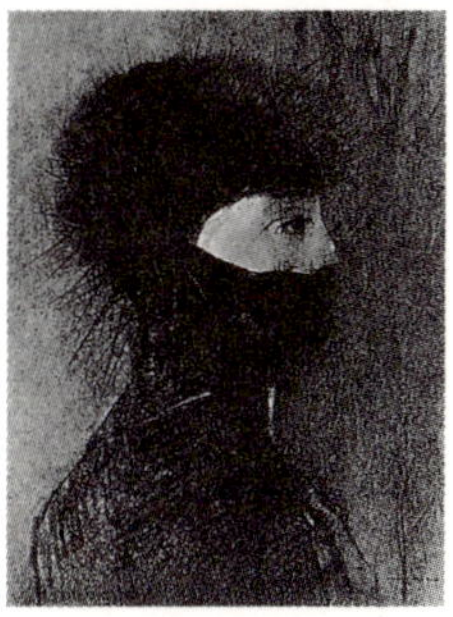

2. Armoured Woman in Profile - 1891. The Metropolitan Museum, New York - *One of the many creatures of Redon's imagination. The strong contrast between black and white accentuates the mystery of this closed-in figure. Perhaps the artist wants to suggest that there is something inaccessible about women or perhaps the meaning is something completely different. Redon never reveals exactly what he is thinking.*

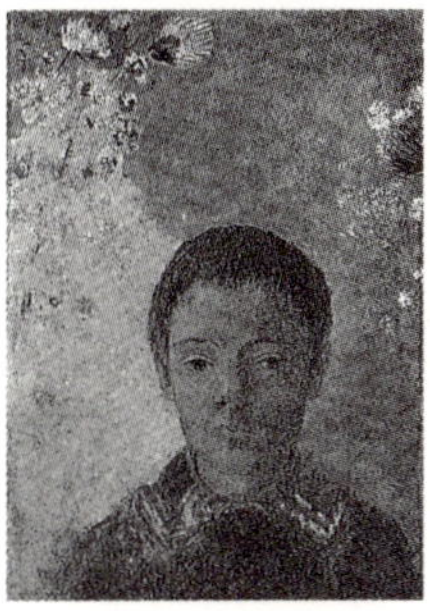

3. Portrait of the Artist's Son Ari - 1897. The Art Institute of Chicago - *The period of the "black pictures" is over ("I just couldn't do them any more," he confessed). Now he loves light and colour and uses pastels for his portraits. In this portrait the pastels enable him to give "soul" to the portrayal of the young boy and delicate freshness to the background.*

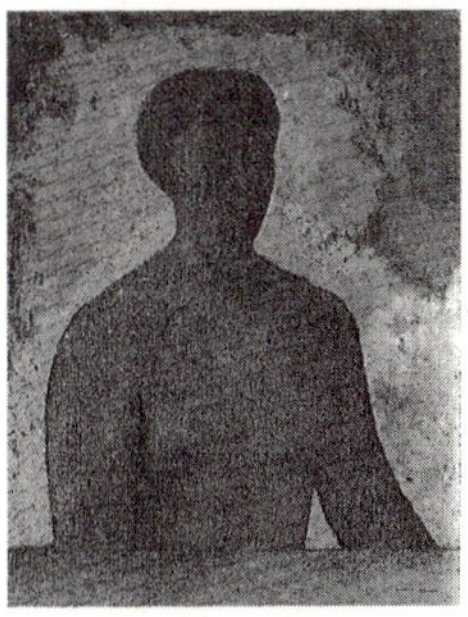

4. Eve - 1904. Musée du Louvre, Paris. - *"Which is more vast in this world, mountains or women?" asked Redon in his diary* A' soi-meme *(To himself). Having reached artistic maturity, he is able to extend his love of the harmony of nature to the harmony of the female body. He loved painting nudes and produced some extremely impressive canvases.*

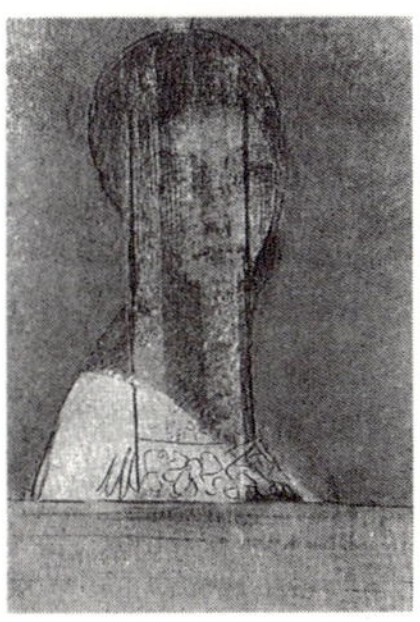

5. The Veil - 1895 ca. Rijksmuseum Kröller-Müller, Otterlo. - *Mystery and woman: two themes very close to Redon's heart. On a warm, delicate background, achieved by means of the use of pastel, we see a female figure with large eyes and an intense expression. But a veil separates us from her thoughts.*

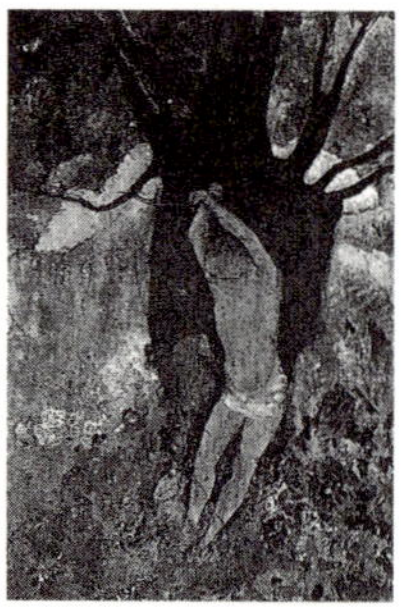

6. Saint Sebastian - 1901. Offentliche Kunstsammlung, Basel. - *The martyred saint leans against a tree and becomes one with nature. The human world and the natural world have the same life and the same feelings. The branches of the tree appear to be arms lifted in despair while the blurred foliage of the thicket seems to be ready to receive the saint's young body.*

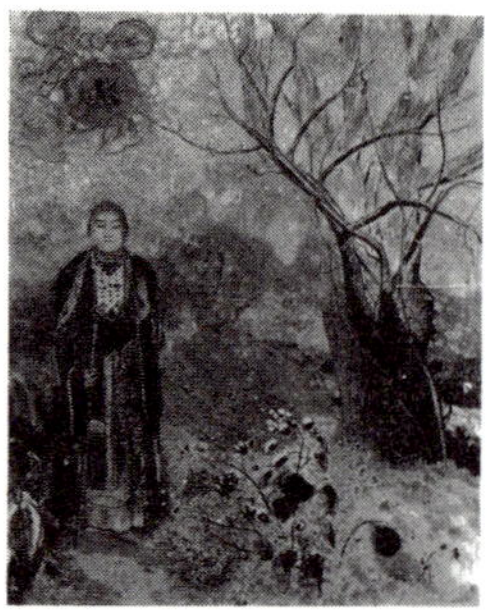

7. Buddha - 1905. Musée d'Orsay, Paris. - *Already represented in two lithographs of 1894 and 1895, the master of meditation reappears in this pastel drawing of 1905. He is standing in a garden where naturalistic elements mingle with certain unreal touches. The tree could be found in the countryside near Peyrelebade, where Redon spent his childhood, but the flowers would be more at home in an earthly paradise.*

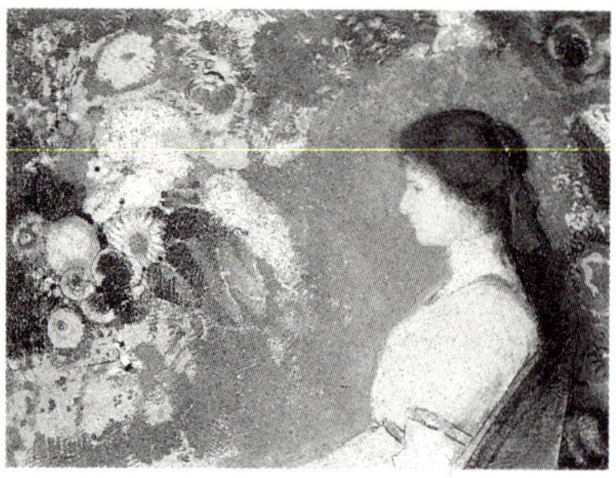

8. Portrait of Mademoiselle Violette Heymann - 1909. Museum of Art, Cleveland. - *A special light illuminates the face of the young Violette. The special atmosphere comes from Redon's use of pastel effects. The girl seems to be part of cosmic life as flowers and butterflies participate in her thoughts and her spirituality.*

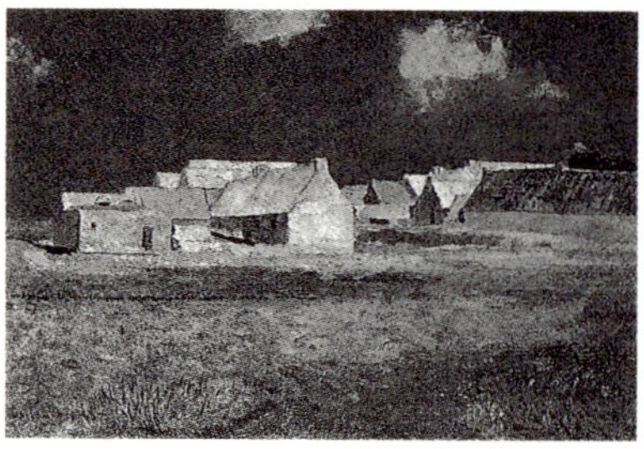

9. Breton Village - before 1890. Paul Mellon Collection, USA. - *During his travels Redon produced many landscapes painted in the open air. When he painted this view of Brittany, faithfully reproducing what he saw, he was still strongly under the influence of the landscape painter Corot. Nevertheless alongside the reality that Redon "sees", there is in the picture also the reality that Redon "feels": the sense of desolation given by a place that is beautiful and yet abandoned.*

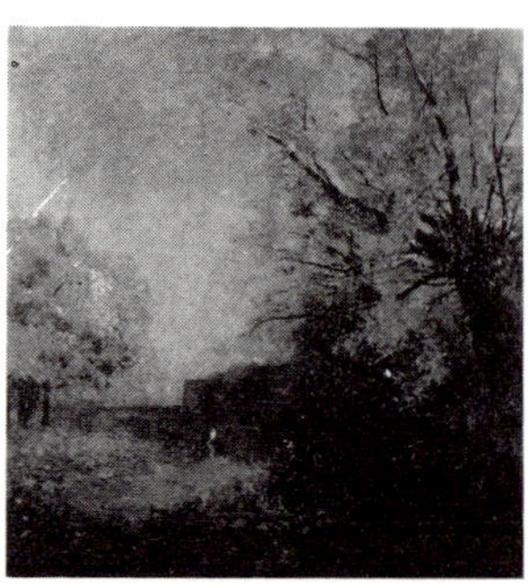

10. Landscape at Peyrelebade - 1880. Private collection, Paris. - *In this oil painting we see the landscape that was the subject of Redon's first dreams: the countryside in which he ran free as a child. Some tall trees around an isolated house and overgrown spaces trodden by hardly anyone except the members of Redon's family.*

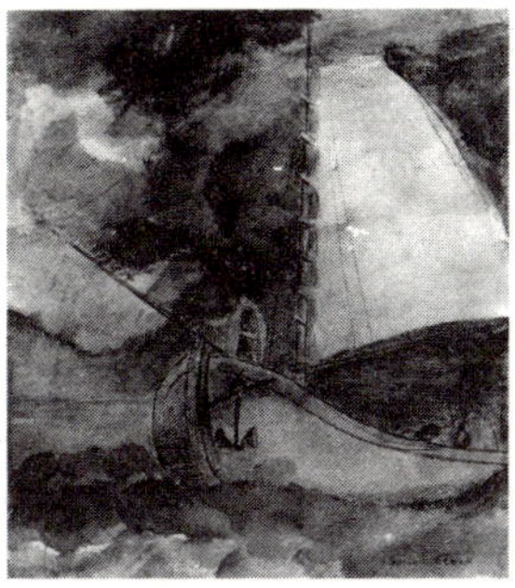

11. Sailing Boat - 1900 ca. Private collection, Paris. - *In this picture Redon used water-colours to depict a seascape. There are people on the boat, but they can hardly be seen at all. The predominant feature is the force of the natural elements to which the people and the boat must submit; the sky is turning red and the waves are choppy. It is a sight that Redon must have seen many times from the top of the Brittany cliffs.*

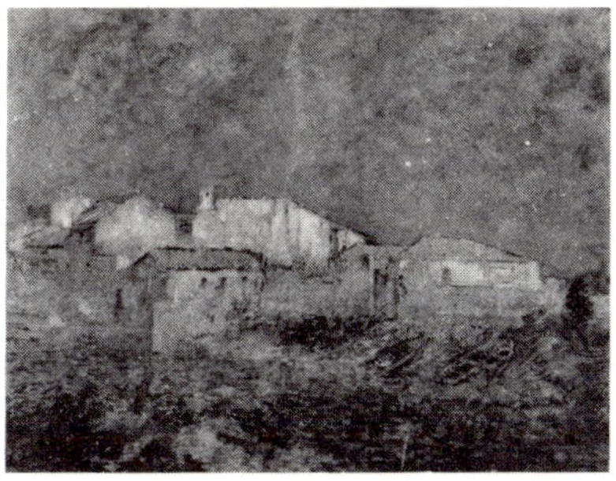

12. View of Venice - after 1908. Musée des Beaux-Arts, Bordeaux. - *The peculiar relationship between the land and the sea in Venice has been well captured here by Redon; the two elements almost become one. The artist first travelled to Italy in 1900 and returned in 1908 when he visited Venice. The freedom of expression is far greater than in the landscapes Redon had painted during the previous decade. It is perhaps one of Redon's most impressionistic works.*

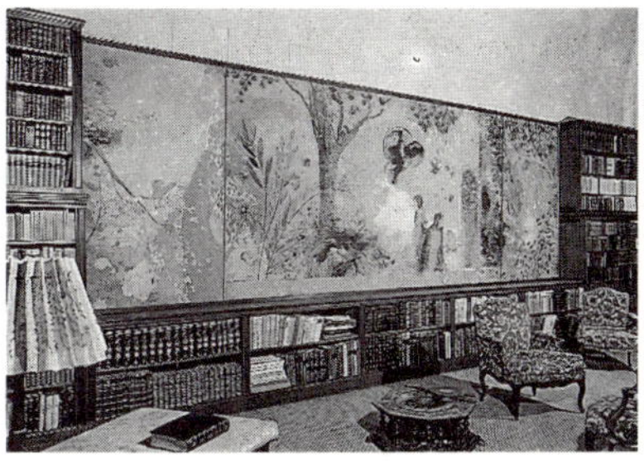

13. The interior of the library at Fontfroide Abbey, near Montpellier. - *Between 1910 and 1911 Redon spent much of his time decorating this library. The work was commissioned by Redon's friend Gustave Fayet, an art collector and the owner of the Abbey. The work, which was carried out during Redon's artistic maturity, is perhaps the greatest of all his achievements.*

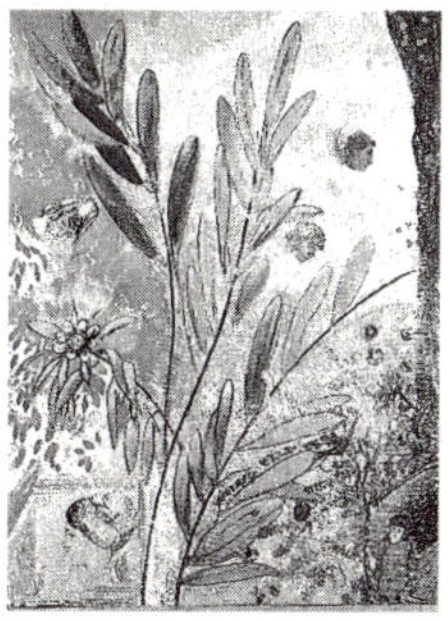

14. Bas-relief: detail of the panel "Night" - Library of Fontfroide Abbey. - *Images from the animal and vegetable kingdoms are mingled together to imply the unity of nature, just as the day mingles with the night.*

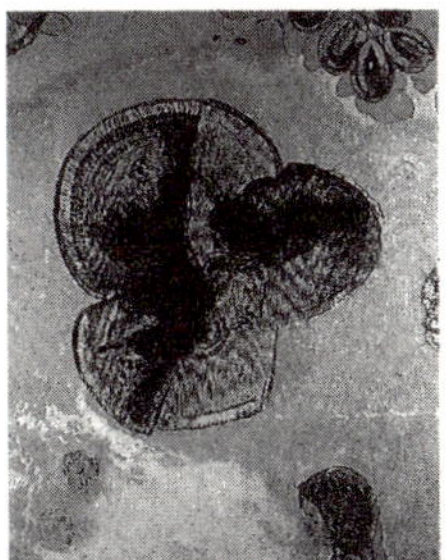

15. The Black Butterfly: detail of the panel "Night" - Library of Fontfroide Abbey. - *Thirty years after the period of the lithographs, which often featured fantastic figures which Redon's critics called "monsters", the artist still enjoys painting these "black" creatures and introduces them as disturbing elements into his evocation of "Night".*

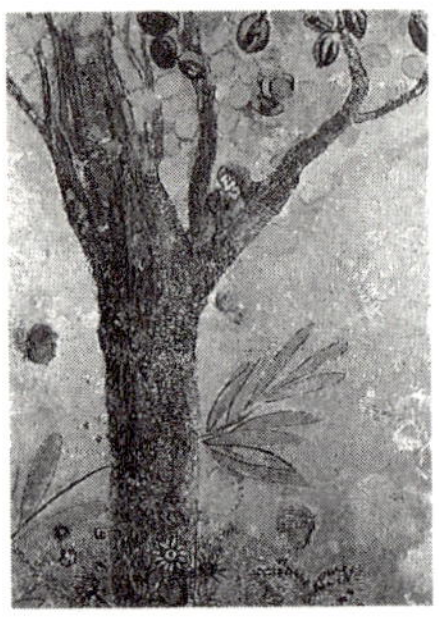

16. Detail of the panel "Night" - Library of Fontfroide Abbey - *A strange creature looks down from a tall tree full of berries and blue flowers; other faces hover about like butterflies. They all contribute to Redon's outstanding evocation of "Night".*

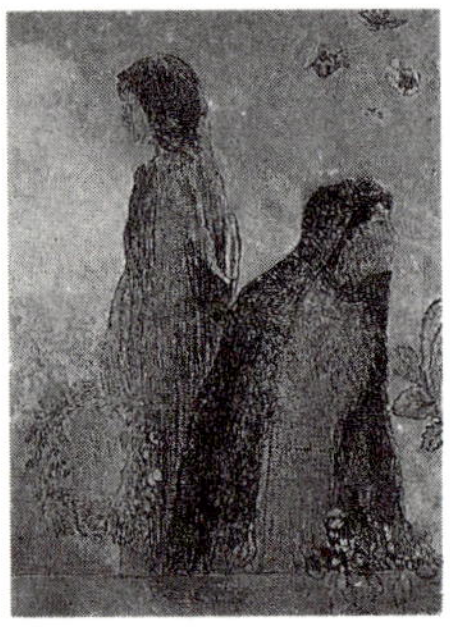

17. Two Women in Mourning: detail of the panel "Night" - Library of Fontfroide Abbey - *Beneath the branches of the tree with the blue flowers, two women dressed in black complete Redon's "Night" and add to its mystery. It is not important to define and specify, Redon used to say, since anything really new and deeply felt bears its own significance.*

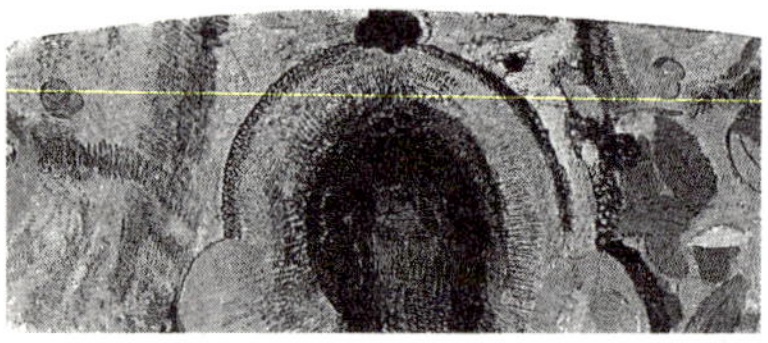

18. Silence: detail of the panel beneath the main entrance - Library of Fontfroide Abbey - *We are invited to silence by this imaginary figure. The invitation is obviously linked to the fact that we are entering a place of study, but it also reflects Redon's need to have silence in order to be able to hear his innermost voice.*

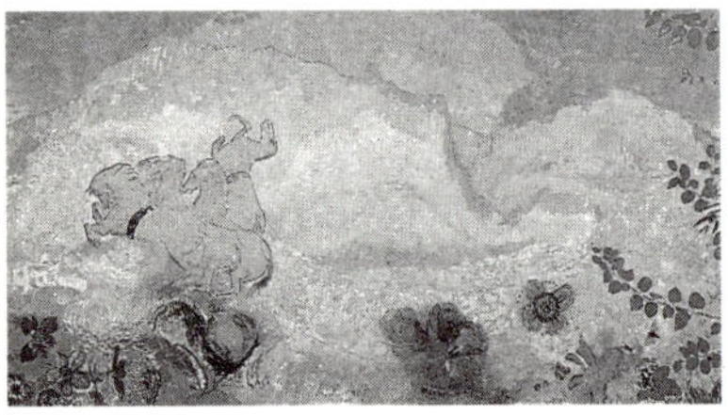

19. Apollo's Sun Chariot: detail of the panel "Day" (central part) - Library of Fontfroide Abbey - *Light and life have triumphed over the night and its phantoms. The mythical chariot of the god of light, with its prancing horses, is like a hymn to the sun and to happiness.*

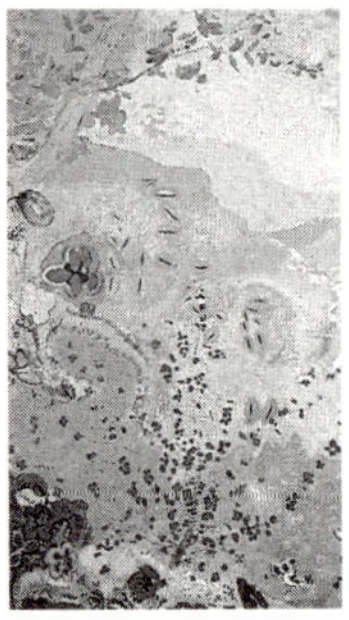

20. Meanders: detail of the panel "Day" (left-hand side) - Library of Fontfroide Abbey - *Redon would never have been able to create this composition of fragments from the plant world without his youthful experiences working with the botanist Armand Clavaud, studying the "infinitely small" and seeing the amazing visions that come to life under the microscope.*

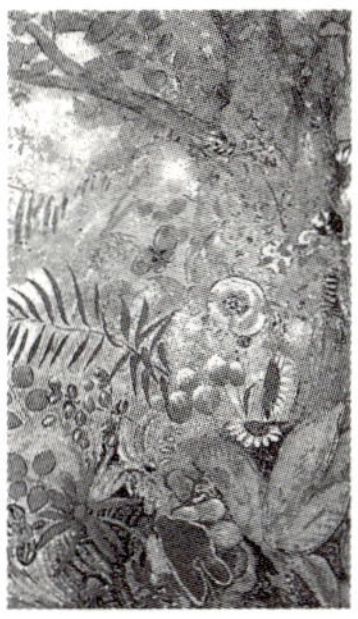

21. Branches and Leaves: detail of the panel "Day" (right- hand side) - Library of Fontfroide Abbey - *A careful observer of nature ever since childhood, Redon studied it carefully and painted it with great attention to detail. His representations of the natural world are, however, never cold or "photographic": he always introduces the fascination of imaginative elements.*

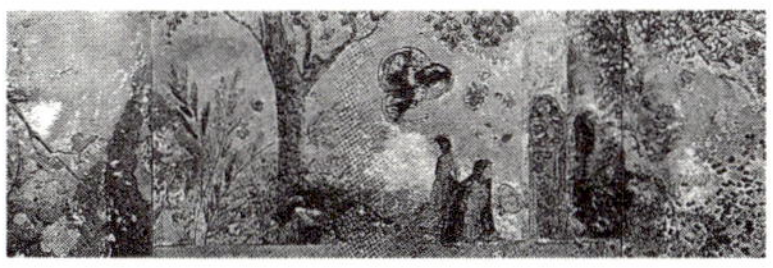

22. The "Night" Panel - 1910-11. Library of Fontfroide Abbey - *Redon used to say that the sombre atmosphere of the Abbey inspired him to melancholy thoughts. Is this the reason for the disturbing figures in the "Night" panel? Maybe. What is certain, however, is that Redon never hesitated about depicting his gloomiest fantasies with great power of expression.*

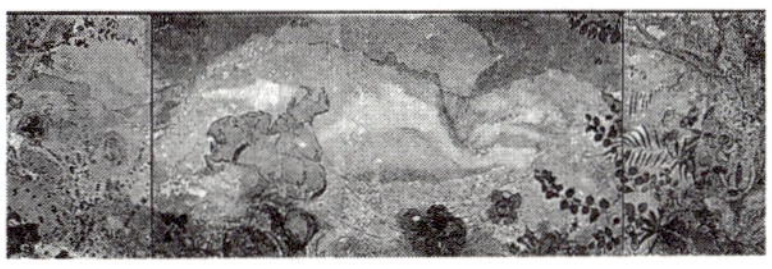

23. The "Day" Panel - 1910-11. Library of Fontfroide Abbey - *When Redon started to decorate the library of Fontfroide Abbey he was already seventy years old. He lived mostly in the South of France, in Cannes, Bièvres or Fontfroide itself, one of the most beautiful spots in the whole of Languedoc. The blazing colours of the "Day" panel were also the result of his contact with these sunlit Mediterranean towns.*

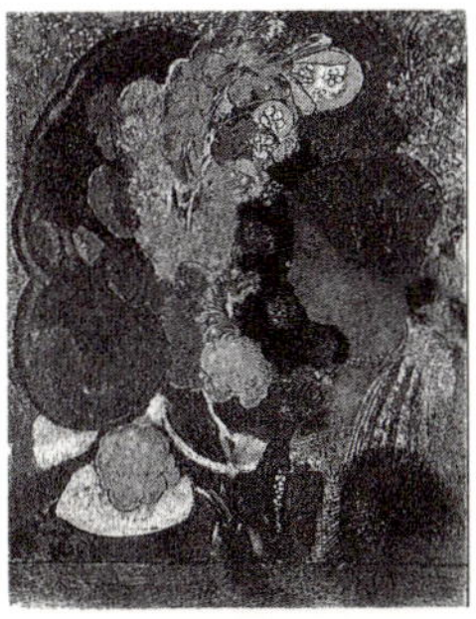

24. Woman Amidst Flowers - 1909-10. Jonas Collection, New York - *Odilon Redon loved women and was fascinated by their beauty and charm. Whenever he drew them, he placed them in a world of flowers, the wild flowers he loved so much. In this pastel drawing the light falls mainly on the flowers so that the face, which is seen in profile and in shadow, acquires a symbolic value.*

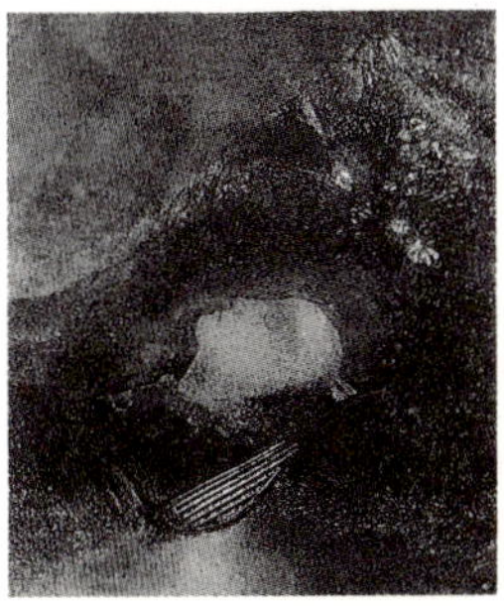

25. Orpheus - 1903 ca. Museum of Art, Cleveland - *When Redon drew this pastel drawing, he had only recently started using colour for his "dreams". Wrapped in a magical atmosphere, Orpheus, the son of Apollo and Caliope, who charmed Charon and Cerberus with his music, is here portrayed as he sleeps.*

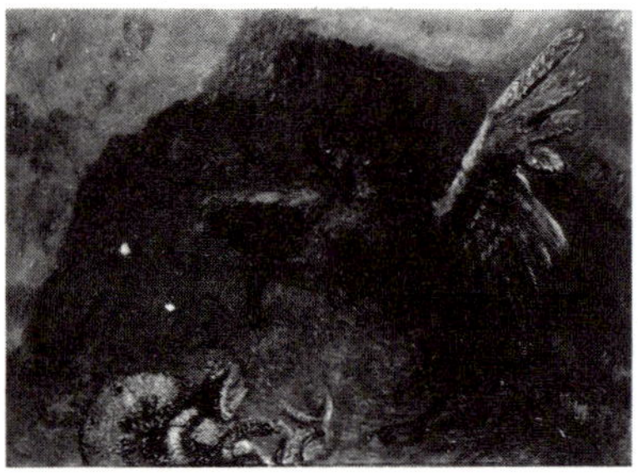

26. Pegasus and the Dragon - 1907 ca. Rijksmuseum Kröller-Müller, Otterlo - *A myth which Redon made his own. Pegasus is the winged horse which triumphed over the dragon and also represents the victory of light and happiness over the artist's past anguish.*

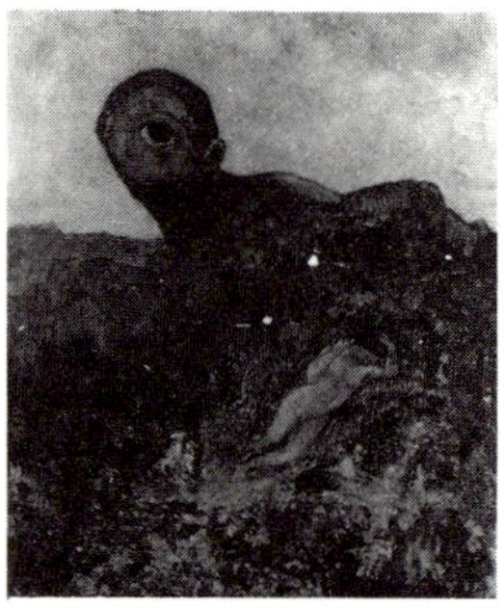

27. Cyclops - 1895-1900. Rijksmuseum Kröller-Müller, Otterlo - *This oil painting on wood was painted during Redon's period of transition from his "black" pictures to his period of light and colour. The dramatic aspect of the theme recalls that of the earlier lithographs. Cyclops appears menacingly from behind the mountain while the woman, curled up like a flower, sleeps unawares.*

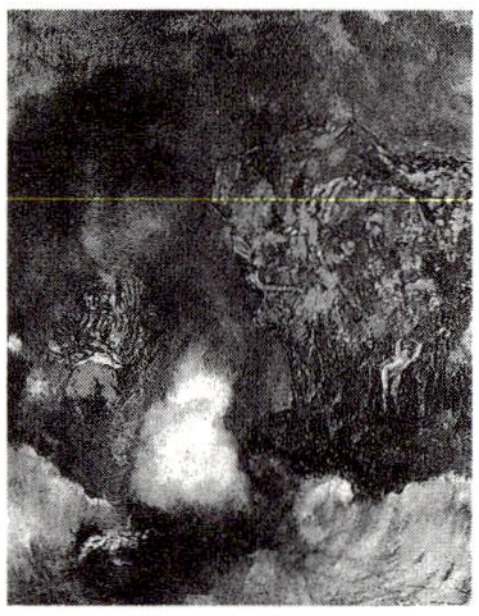

28. Roger and Angelica - 1900 ca. The Museum of Modern Art, Lillie P. Bliss Collection. New York - *The valiant Roger, who has crossed France on his winged horse, looks down into the Brittany sea and spots a very beautiful woman (Angelica) tied to a rock. He decides to rescue her. The canvas, full of both tumult and pathos, does full justice to its mythological theme.*

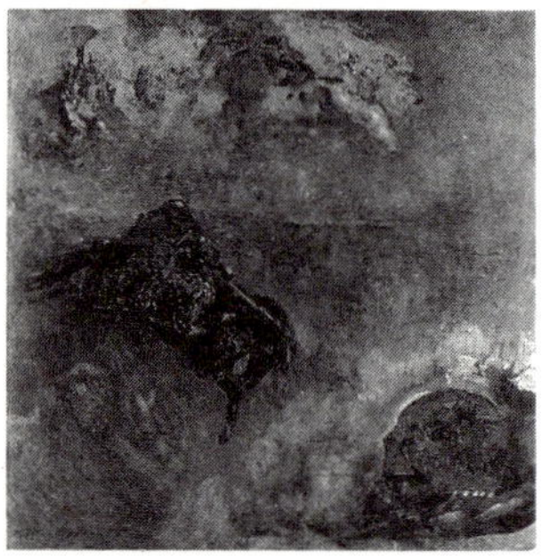

29. Roger and Angelica - 1909-1910. Rijksmuseum Kröller-Müller, Otterlo - *Roger, on his black horse, emerges from the depths of the sea, ready to attack the green sea monster. When he has defeated the monster, he frees Angelica and carries her away on a hippogriff.*

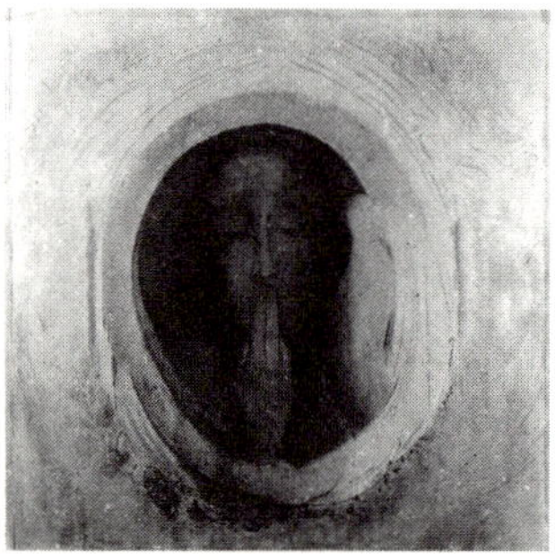

30. Silence (a variation on the decoration at Fontfroide Abbey) - 1911. The Museum of Modern Art, New York - *This oil painting on paper is a repetition of the theme of the painting to be seen on the wall of the library of Fontfroide Abbey. With lowered eyes and a grave expression, the figure invites us to keep silent. What does the figure represent? We'll never know.*

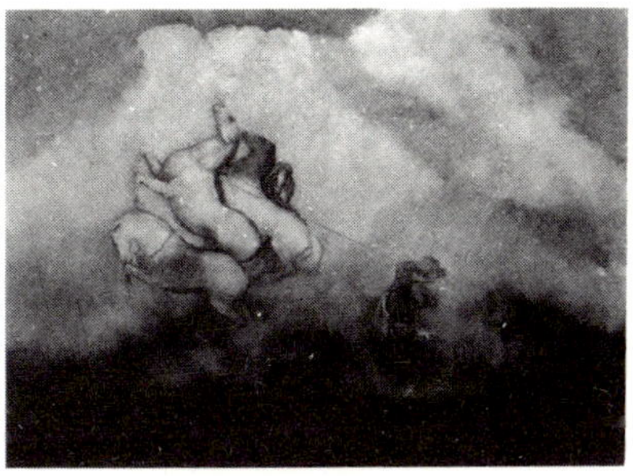

31. Phaeton's Fall - 1910 ca. Private collection, France - *Another myth which adds fuel to Redon's visionary powers: Phaeton, the son of Helios the sun-god, is struck down by Zeus for coming too close to earth in his father's chariot, risking setting the world on fire.*

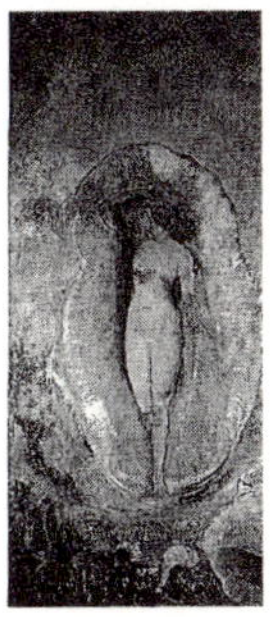

32. The Birth of Venus - 1912. Stephen Higgons collection, Paris - *The human body and the world of nature: two aspects of the same harmony. How better to convey it than this representation of Venus, the goddess of love and beauty, emerging from a shell?*

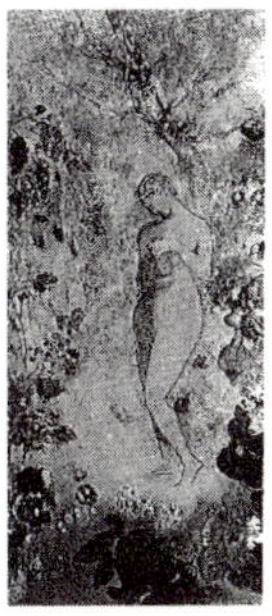

33. Pandora - 1910. The Metropolitan Museum of Art, Alexander M. Bing legacy. New York - *"The female nude should be placed in a Garden of Eden", said Redon, "for eyes that are not ours, but those of an imaginary world where beauty, which is never immodest, is born and multiplied."*

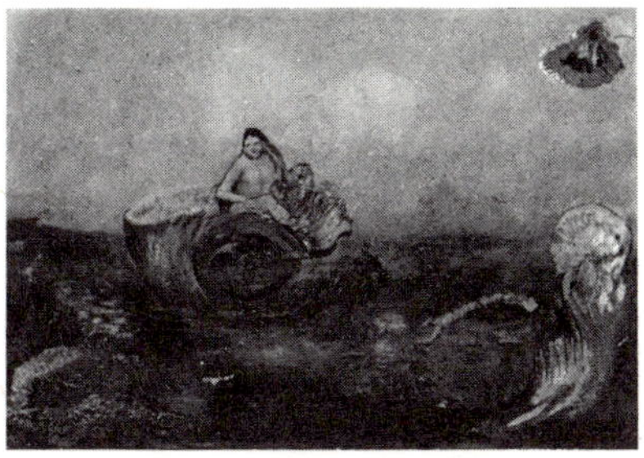

34. The Birth of Venus - 1902. Private collection, USA - *Another representation of Venus on canvas. The goddess is immersed in one of the landscapes which Redon, attracted by the mystery of our origins, loved to dream about: nature is still a thing of the future and anything can happen.*

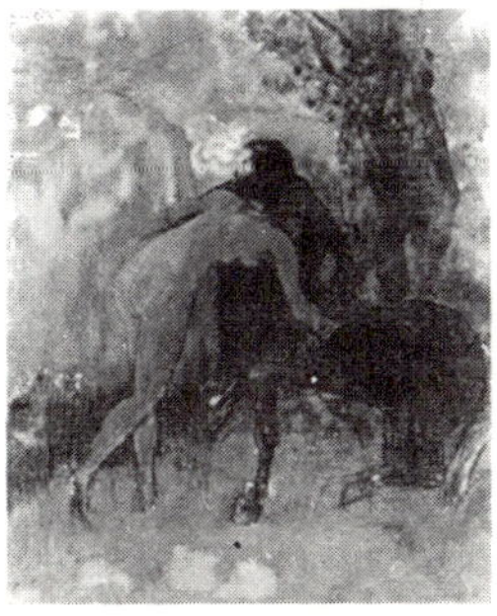

35. Woman and Centaur - 1900-1910. Private collection, France - *The trunk of a tree rising out of the picture: a constant in Redon's landscapes; an enchanted mountain and a warm sky; some aspects of nature invented, others real-this picture is basic to Odilon Redon's poetry.*

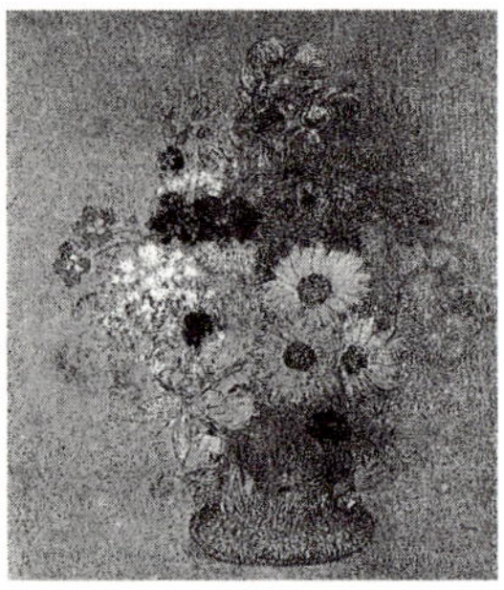

36. Vase of Flowers - Private collection, USA - *The first works devoted to flowers are dated 1900: Redon's "colour" period has just started. For this type of composition he preferred to use pastels and the flowers he uses as "models" are almost always wild flowers.*

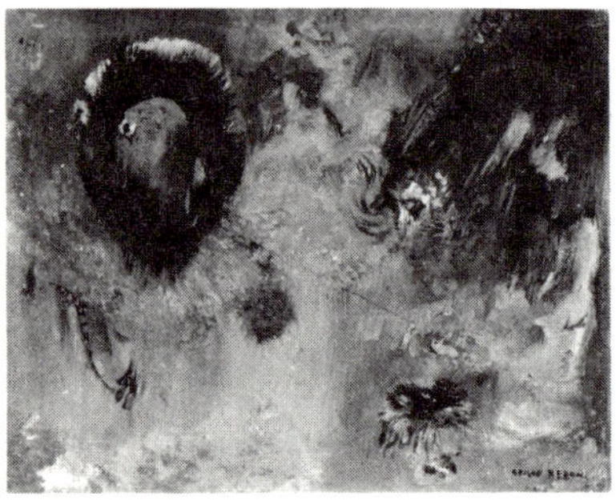

37. Phantasmagoria - Musée des Beaux-Arts, Bordeaux - *A universe in formation, with no clear distinction as yet between the animal and vegetable kingdoms. This theme was dear to Redon and goes back to the days when he studied nature with the scientist Clavaud and was a young pupil of the visionary Rodolphe Bresdin.*

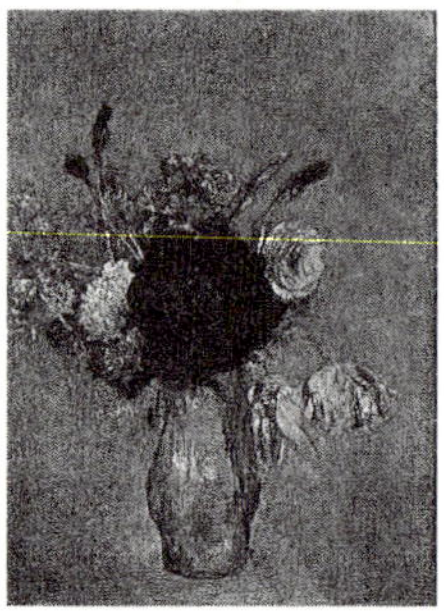

38. Vase of Flowers - Private collection, USA - *In the same way that he gives a soul to a face or a nude, Redon manages to give spirituality to flowers, one of the favourite subjects of his artistic maturity. For him they represent the positive aspects of growth and coming to flower. Redon's love of "real" flowers, i.e. wild flowers, is also a question of the tenderness he feels for them as a result of their fragility.*

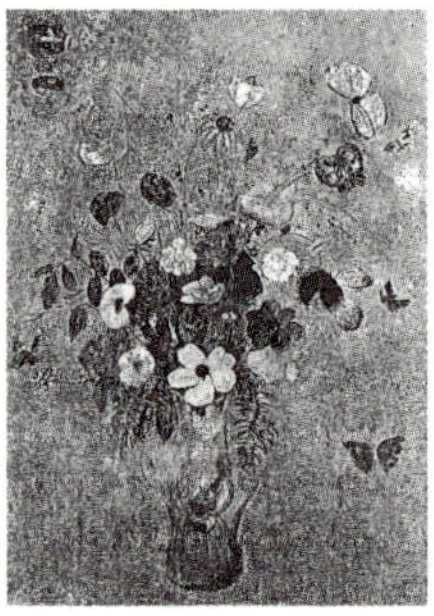

39. Vase with Flowers and Butterflies - Private collection, USA - *There is an explosion of vitality and colour in this painting. The vase is merely a pretext; the whole atmosphere (including the butterflies) is one of an open field of flowers. This is a happy moment in Redon's life and there is no trace of any conflict.*

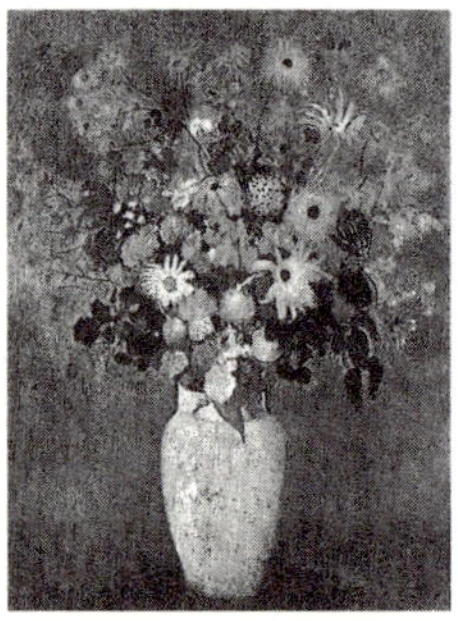

40. Vase of Flowers - 1912 ca. Musée du Louvre, Paris - *An electric current seems to be running through the multicoloured flowers in this pastel drawing. Francis Jammes, a young friend of Redon's and a great poet, wrote an article entitled "Odilon Redon the botanist", where he imagines that in Redon's studio he asks a rose the secret of genius. "I don't know," replies the rose, "and neither does he."*

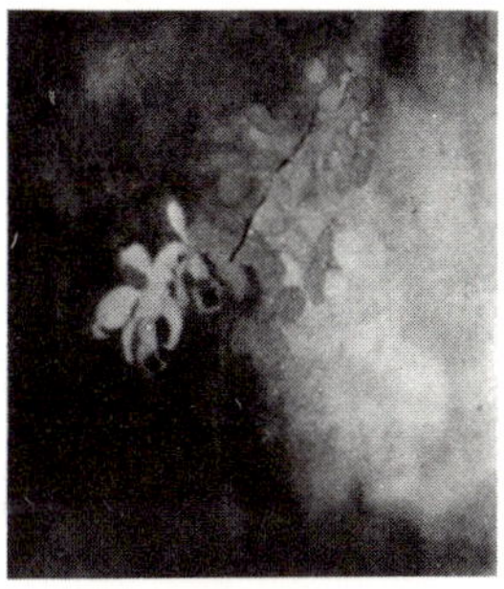

41. Orchid - 1912 ca. Private collection, USA - *Perhaps this pastel drawing is a reply to his friend's question, further proof of his expressive talents. The words spoken by the rose, or rather by Jammes, had shocked him. He knew what he was doing: it was he who was in charge of his brush as he painted. It was his skill that was solely responsible for the results.*

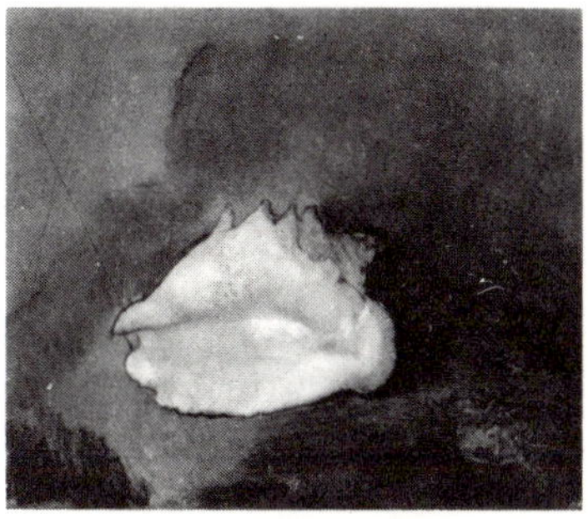

42. Shell - 1912. Private collection, Paris - *This pastel drawing is a life-size representation of a shell. The shell was a real one: the same one that he had used for his "Birth of Venus" and which his son Ari had kept for years on the mantelpiece at home. Here, however, it has been transfigured and, as beautiful as it is, it is no longer merely an element of nature.*

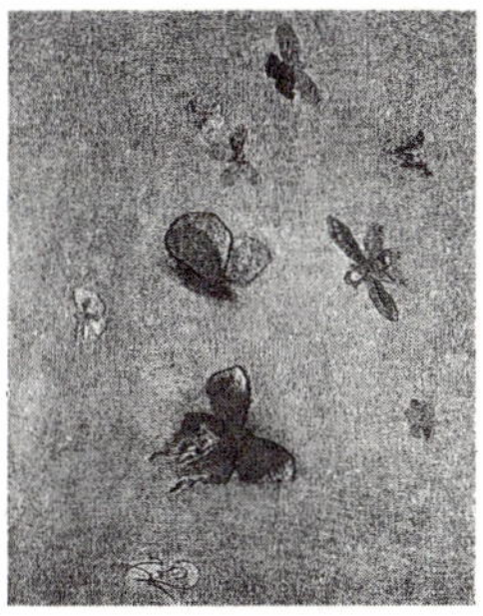

43. Butterflies - 1910 ca. Private collection, USA - *Butterflies set Redon's imagination on fire. They appear in many of his works and at times undergo disturbing metamorphoses. In this composition, however, there are no hidden phantoms. The butterflies fly freely over the canvas, each with its own particular kind of beauty.*

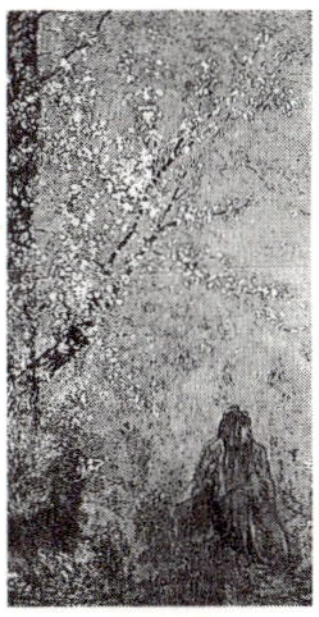

44. The Red Tree - 1906. Private collection - *The use of tempera makes the blossom on the tree look like precious pearls. The tree, which is as tall as those he knew during his childhood years at Peyrelebade, again rises out of the picture. This is a sign of force and stability that contrasts with the anxiety of the figure sitting beneath, whose identity we shall never know.*

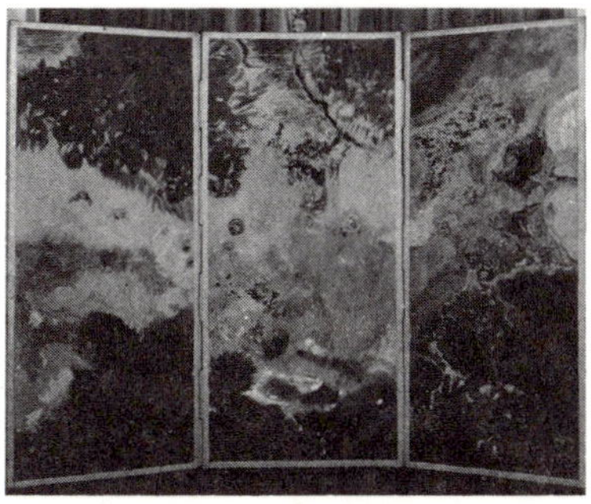

45. The Red Screen - 1906-1908. Private collection - *Redon accepted work on commission even before his decoration of Fontfroide Abbey. His work, however, was never purely decorative: he always found room for his visions. Here we have a whole cosmic universe, painted in tempera on a folding screen.*

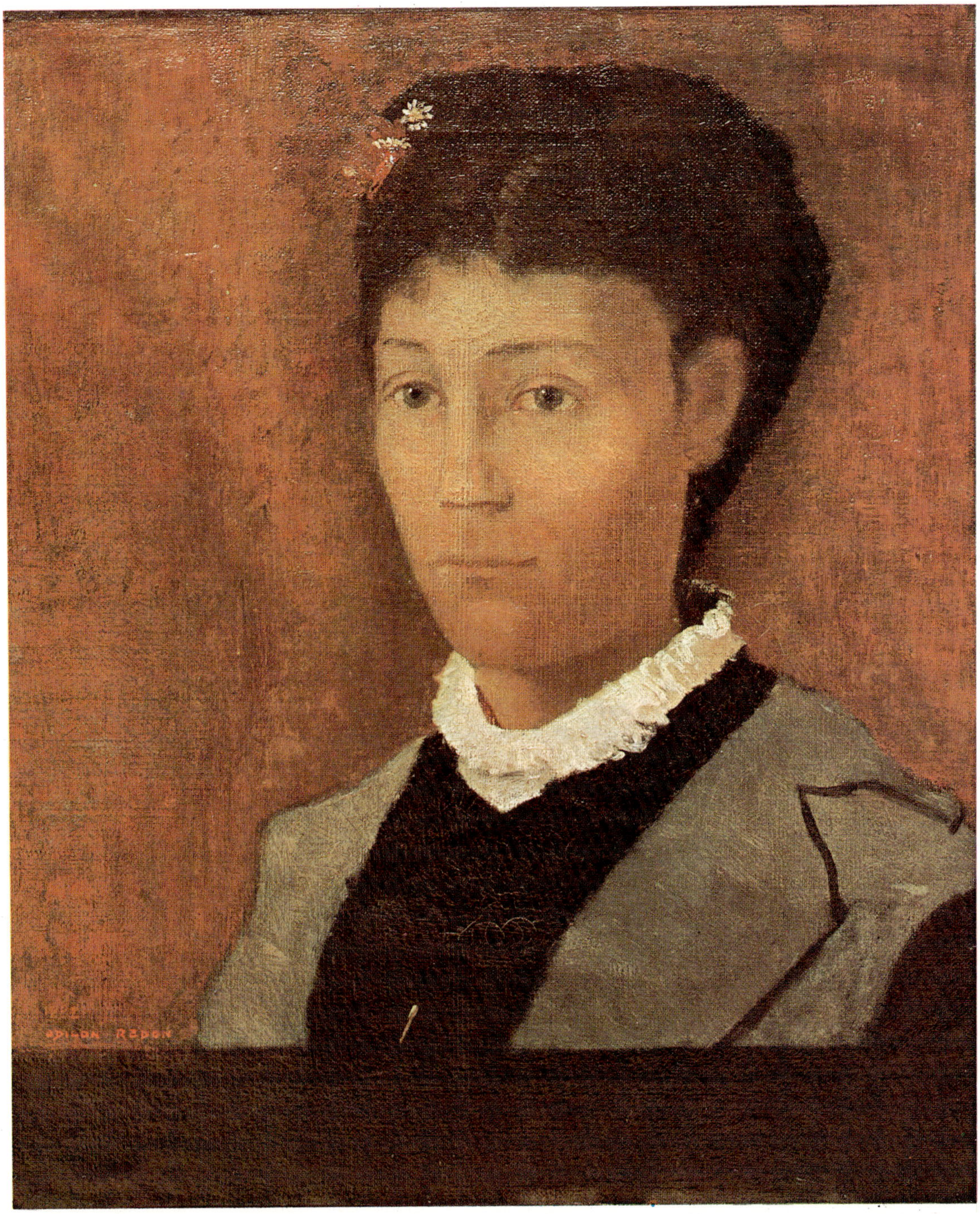

1. *Madame Redon* - 1882. Musée du Louvre, Paris.

2. *Armoured Woman in Profile* - 1891. The Metropolitan Museum, New York.

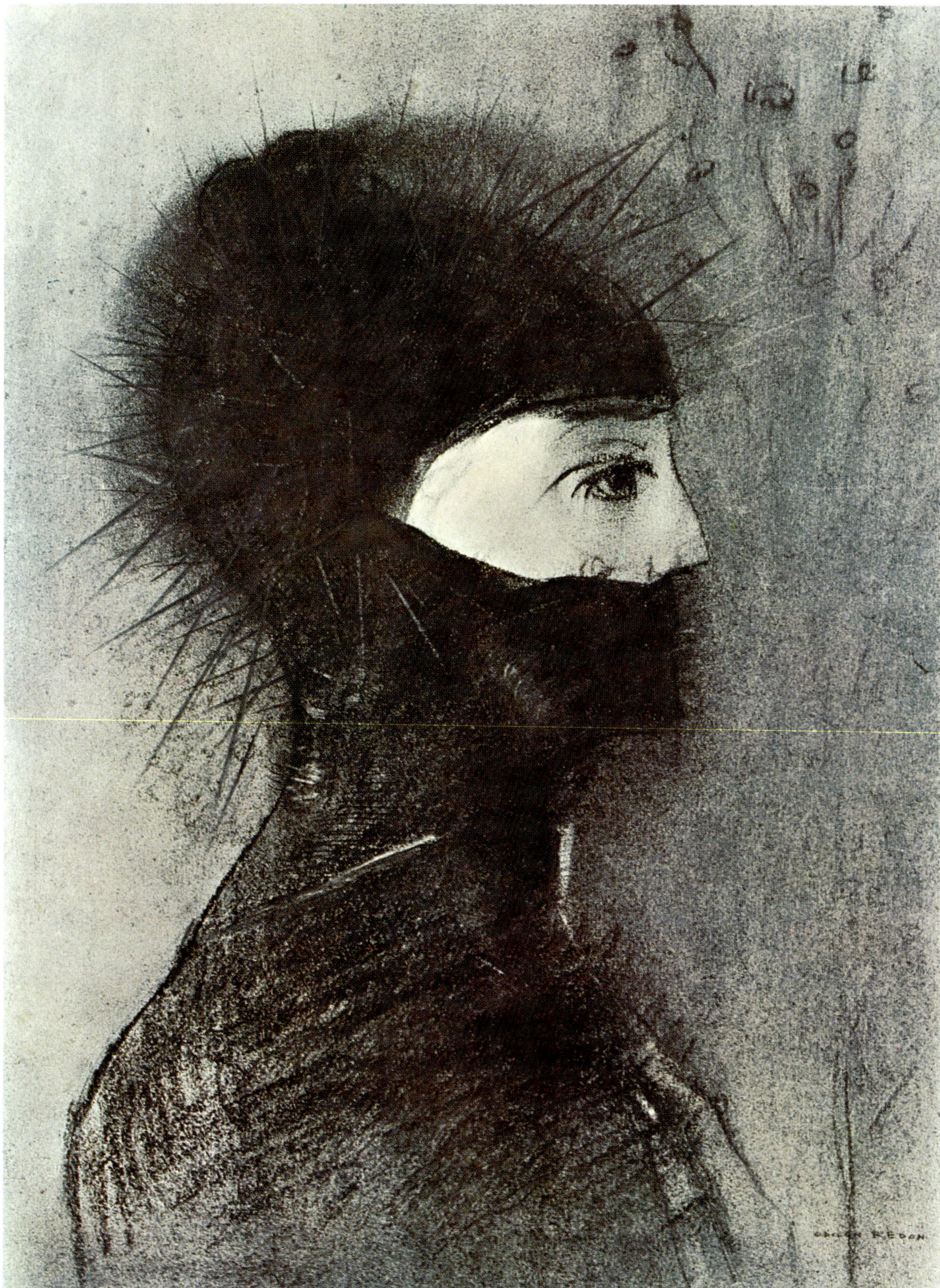

3. *Portrait of the Artist's Son Ari* - 1897.
The Art Institute of Chicago.

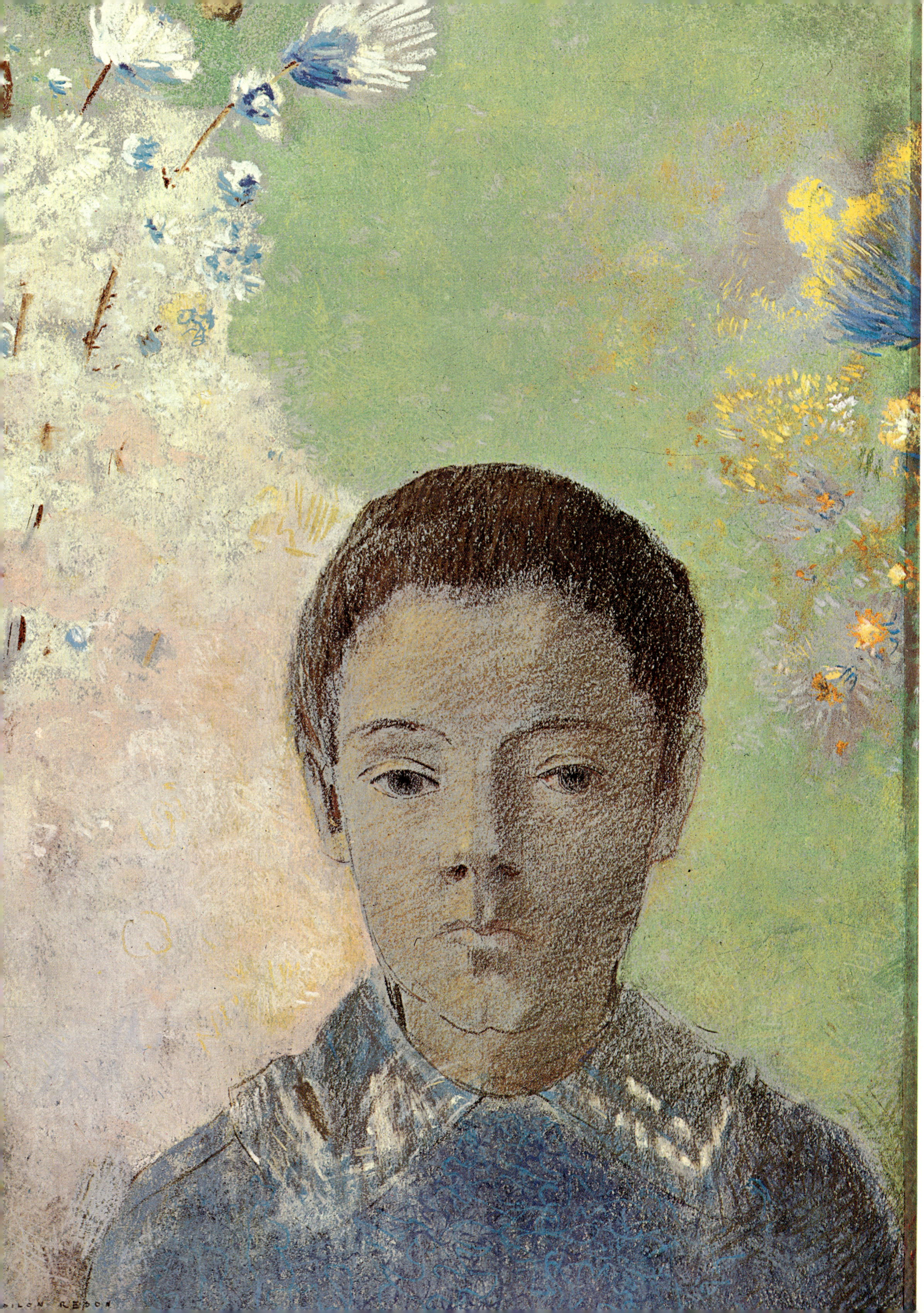

4. *Eve* - 1904. Musée du Louvre, Paris.

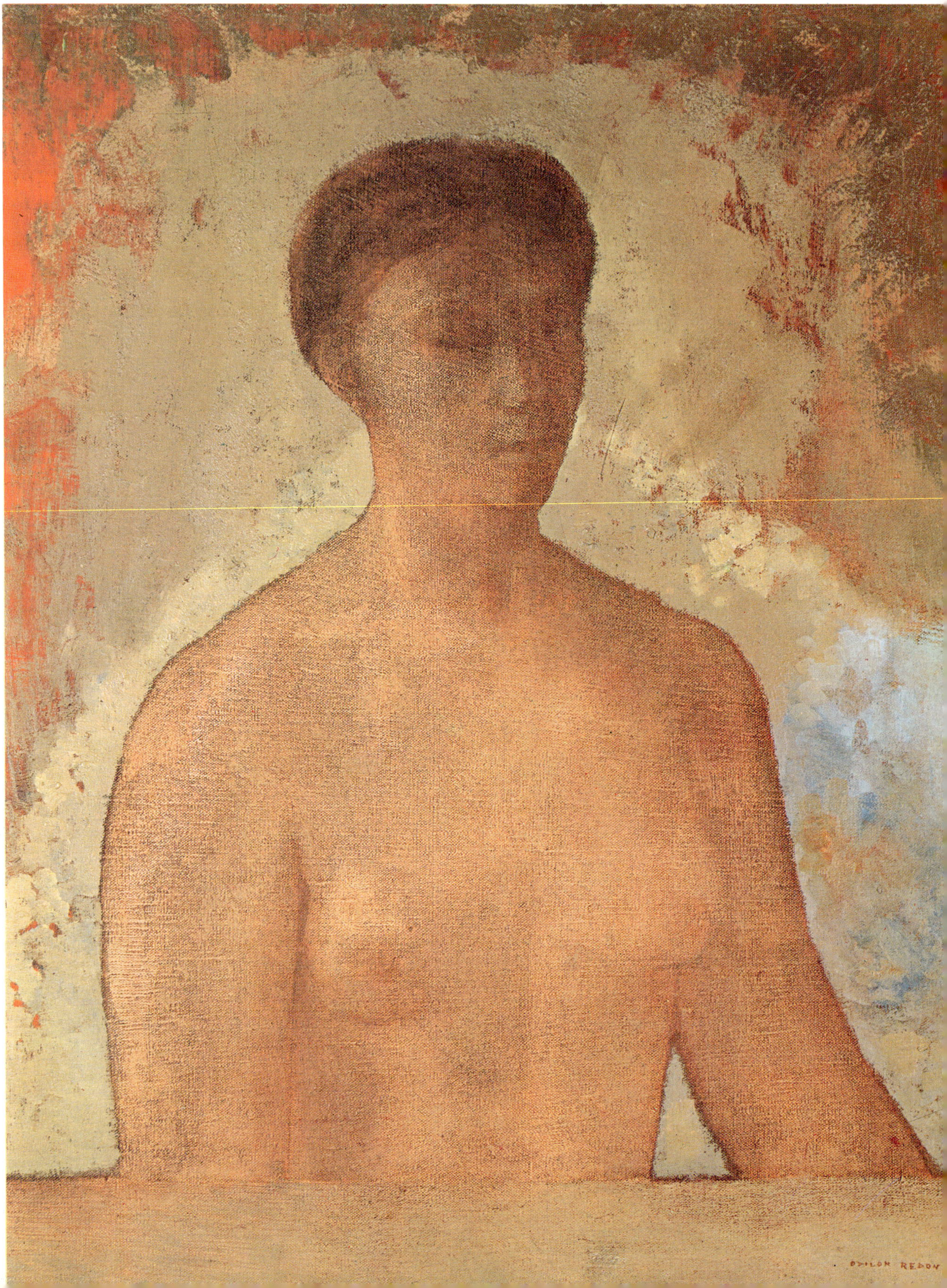

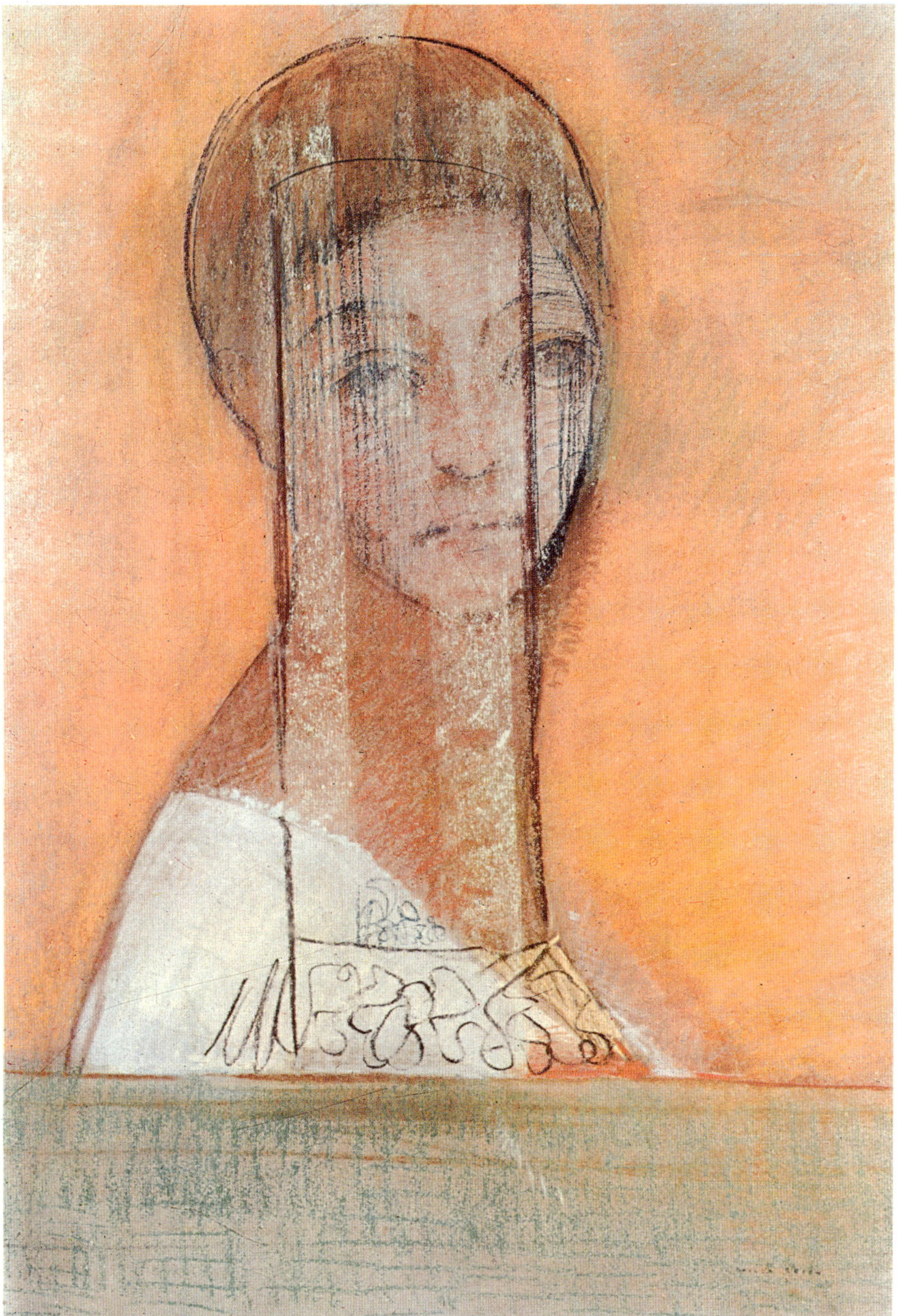

5. *The Veil* - 1895 ca. Rijksmuseum Kröller-Müller, Otterlo.

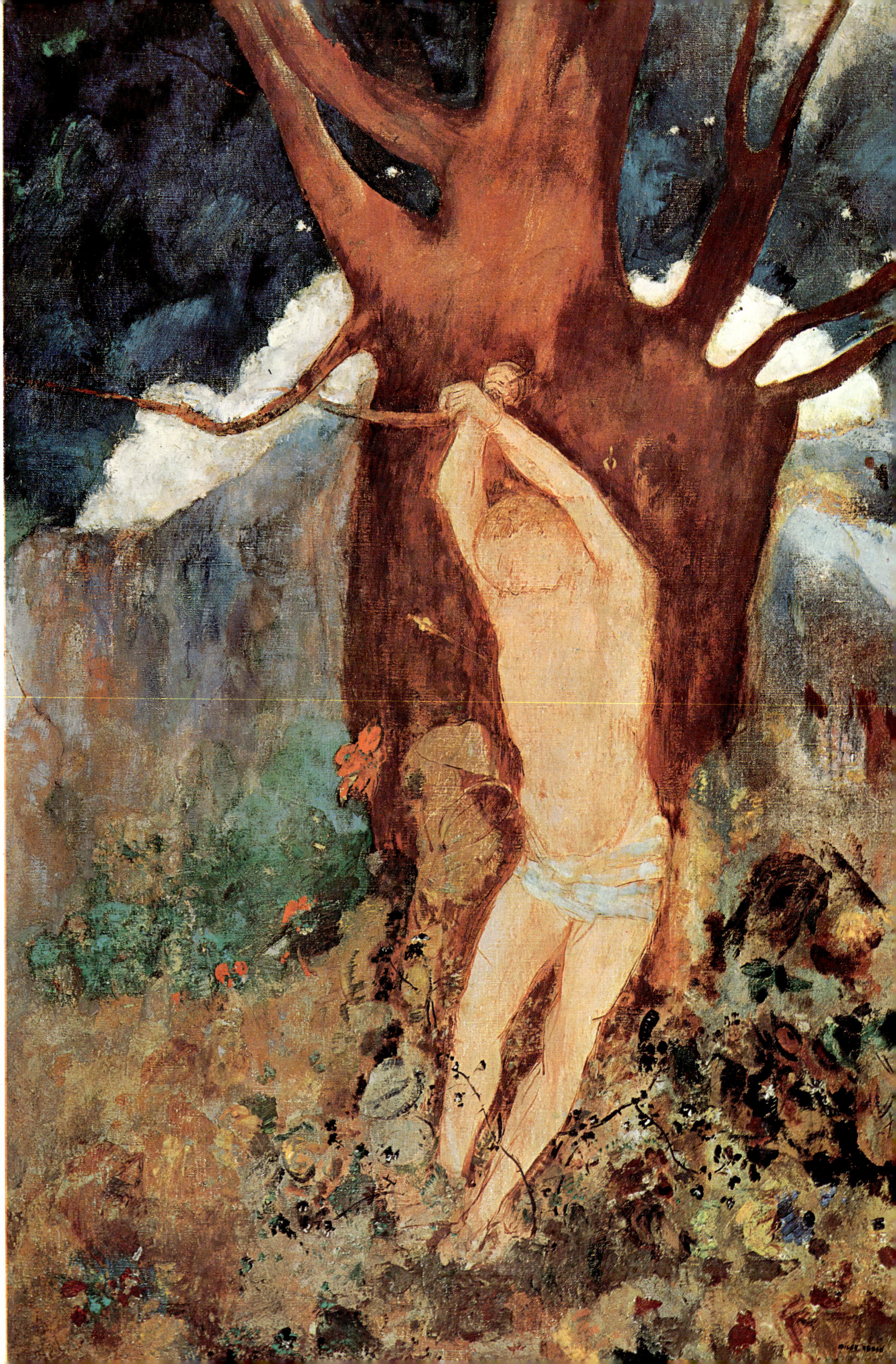

6. *Saint Sebastian* - 1901. Offentliche Kunstsammlung, Basel.

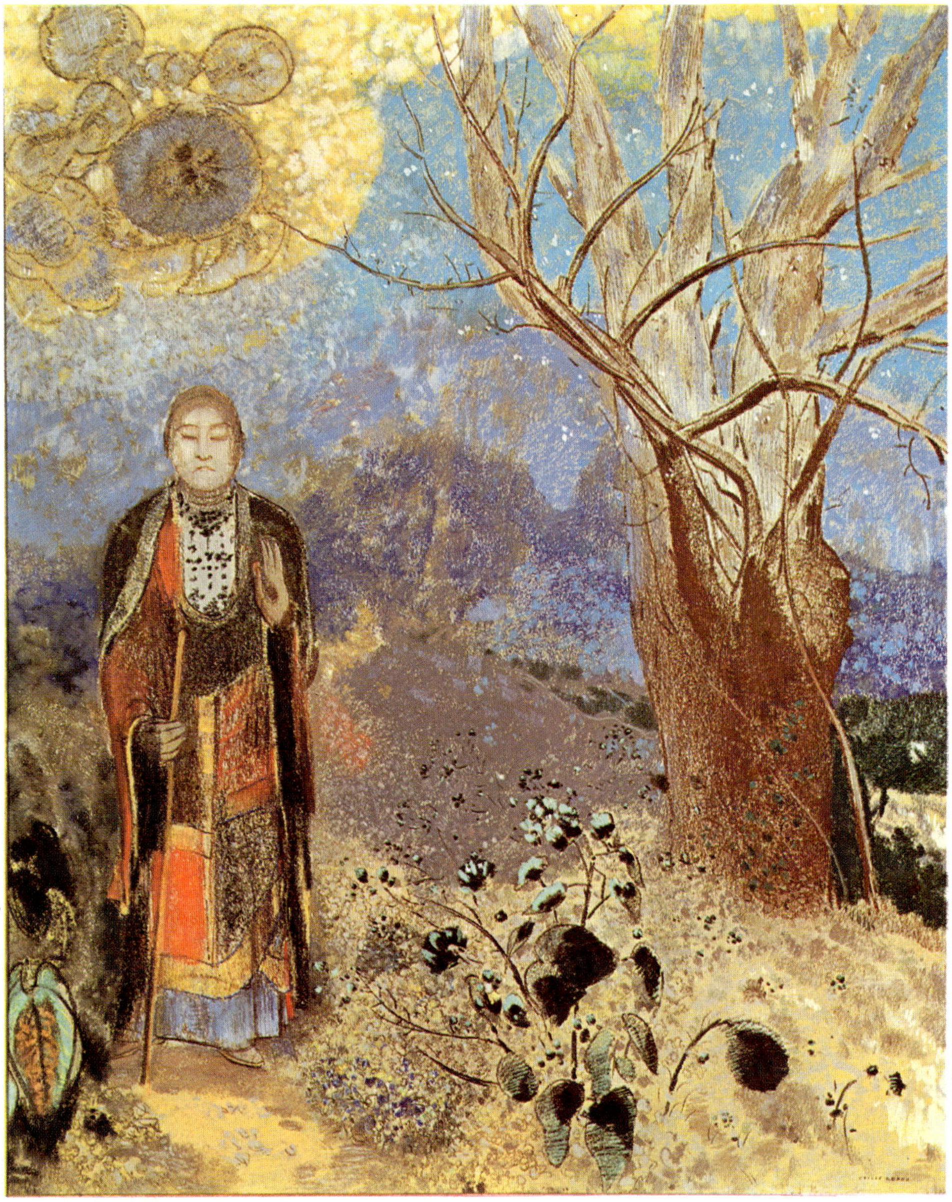

7. *Buddha* - 1905. Musée d'Orsay, Paris.

8. *Portrait of Mademoiselle Violette Heymann* - 1909.
Museum of Art, Cleveland.

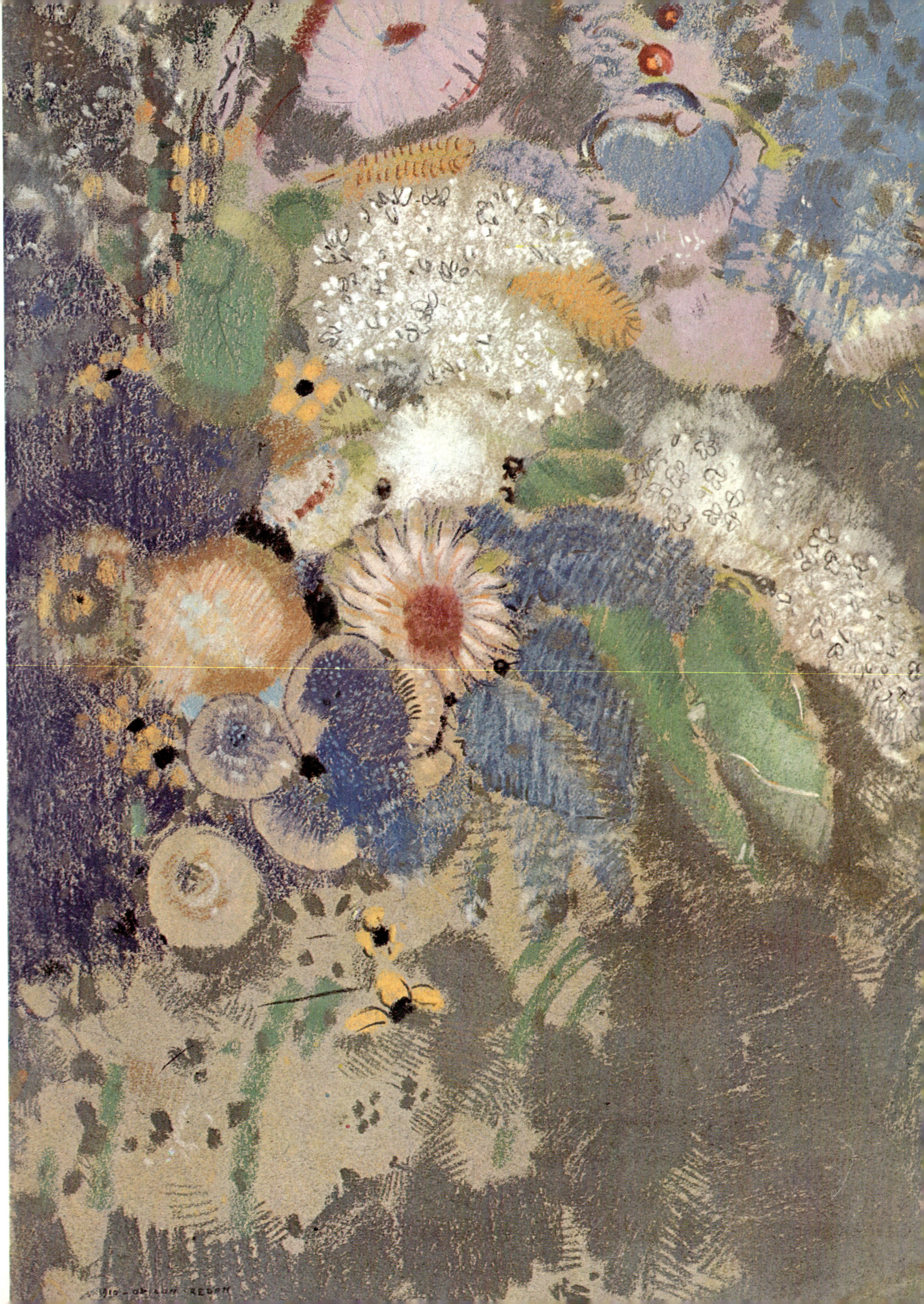

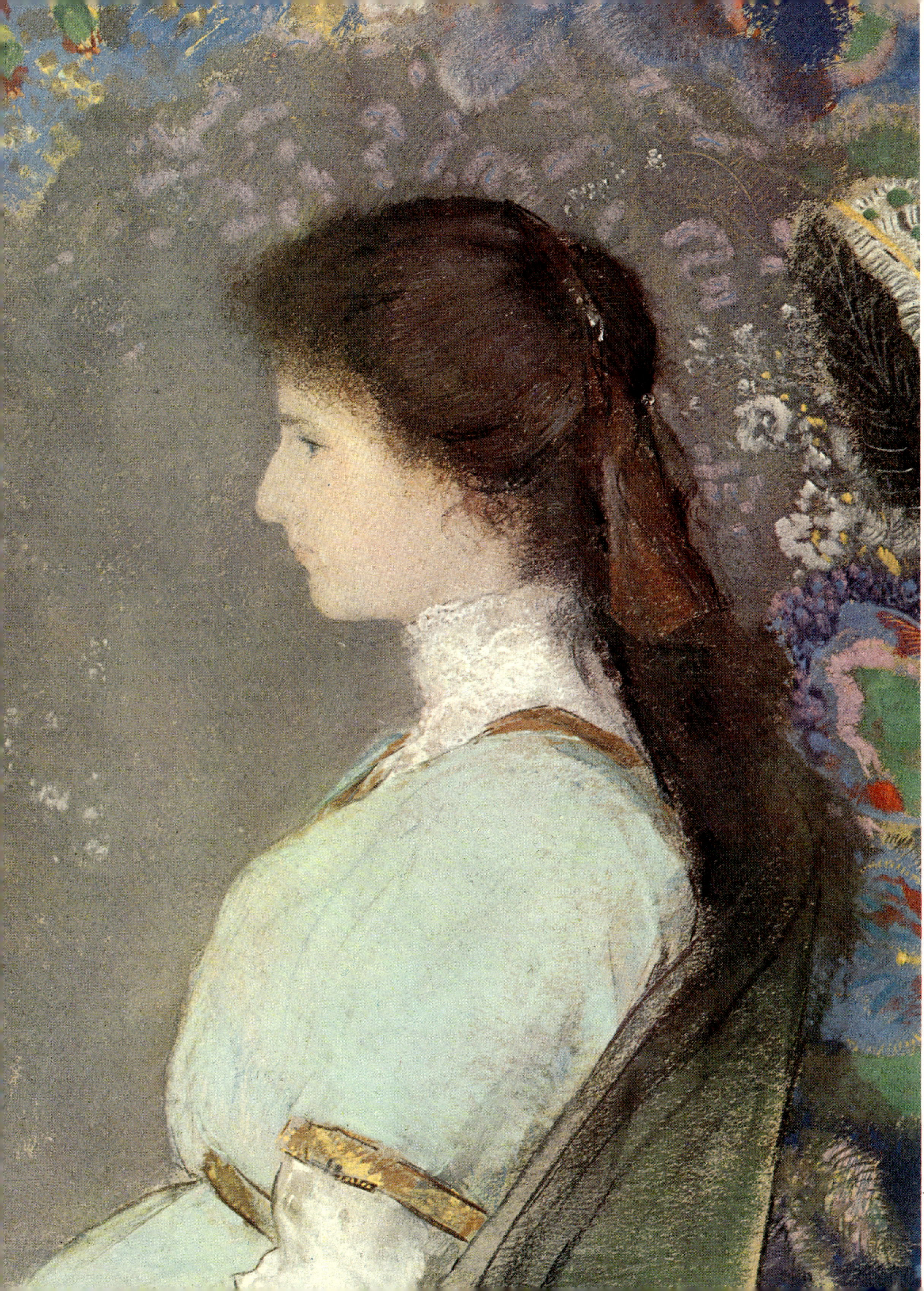

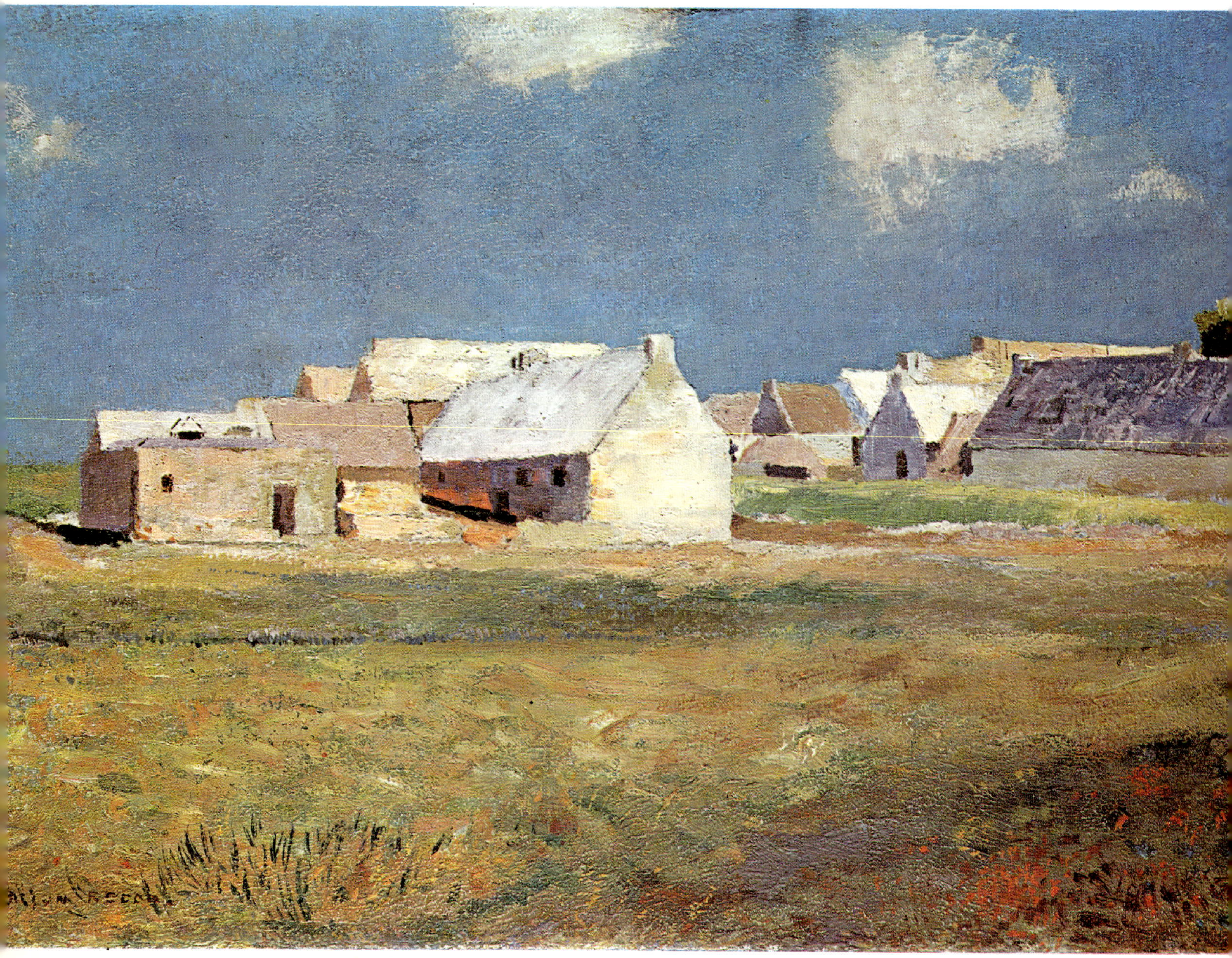

9. *Breton Village* - before 1890. Paul Mellon Collection, USA.

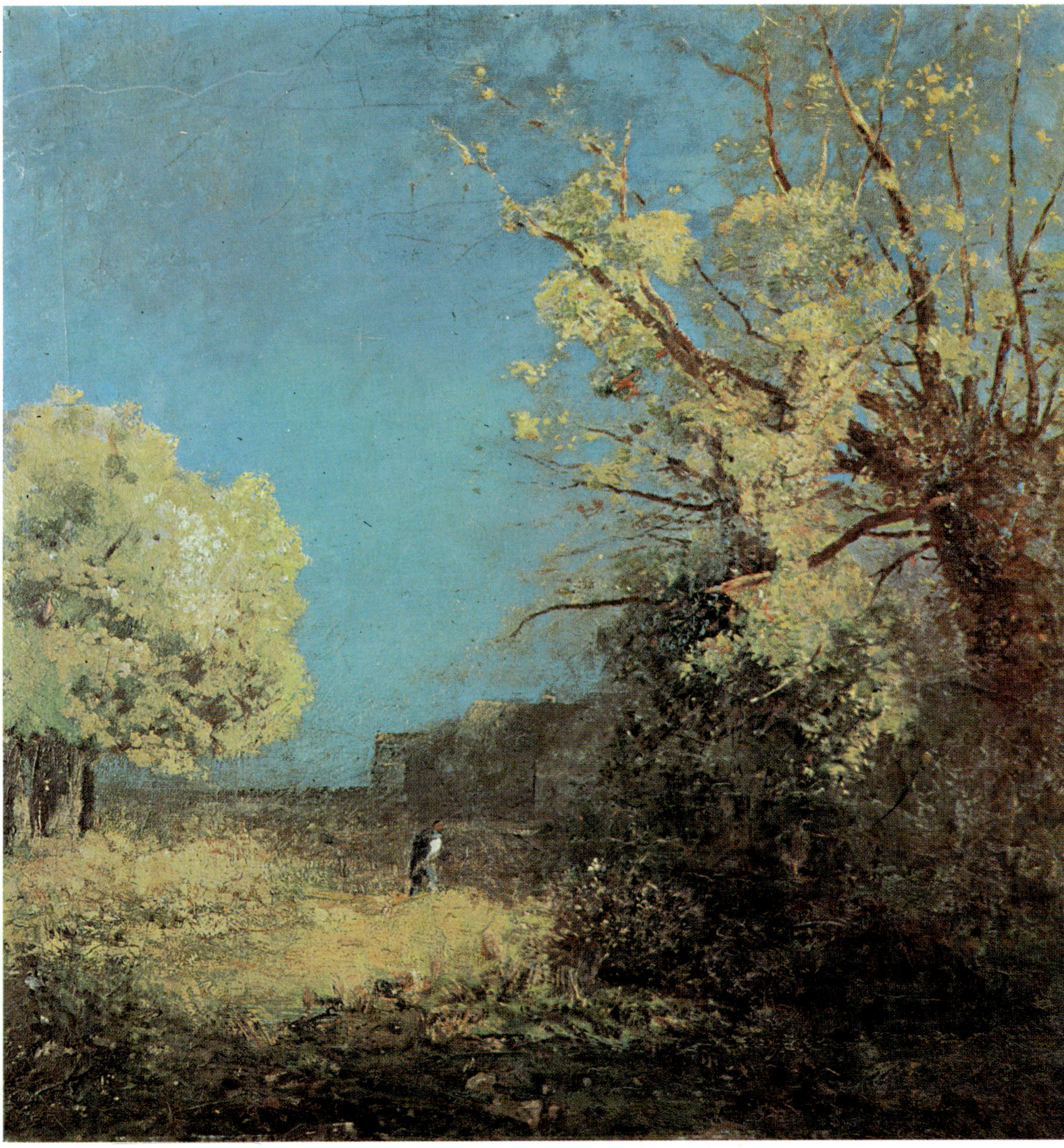

10. *Landscape at Peyrelebade* - 1880. Private collection, Paris.

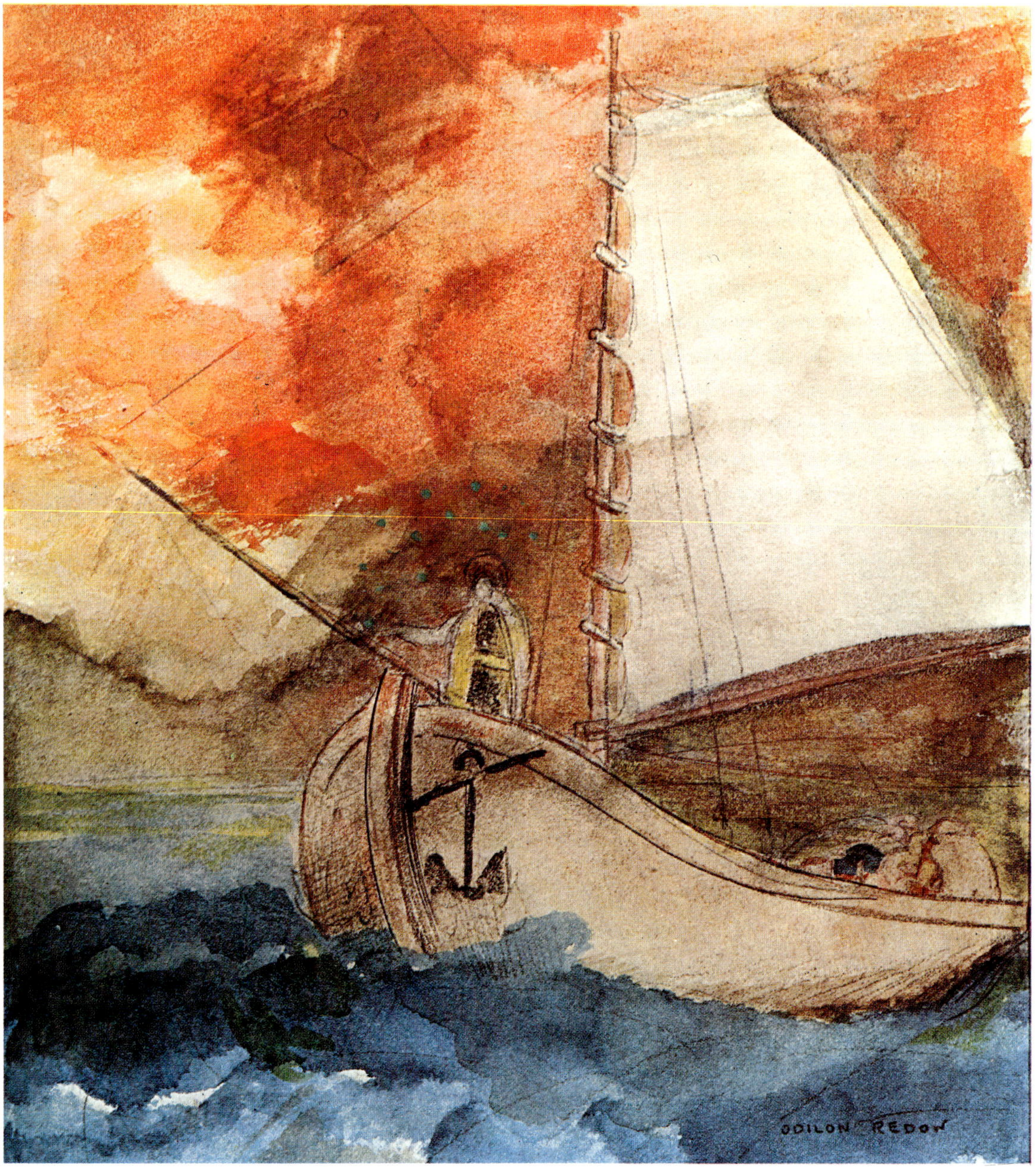

11. *Sailing Boat* - 1900 ca. Private collection, Paris.

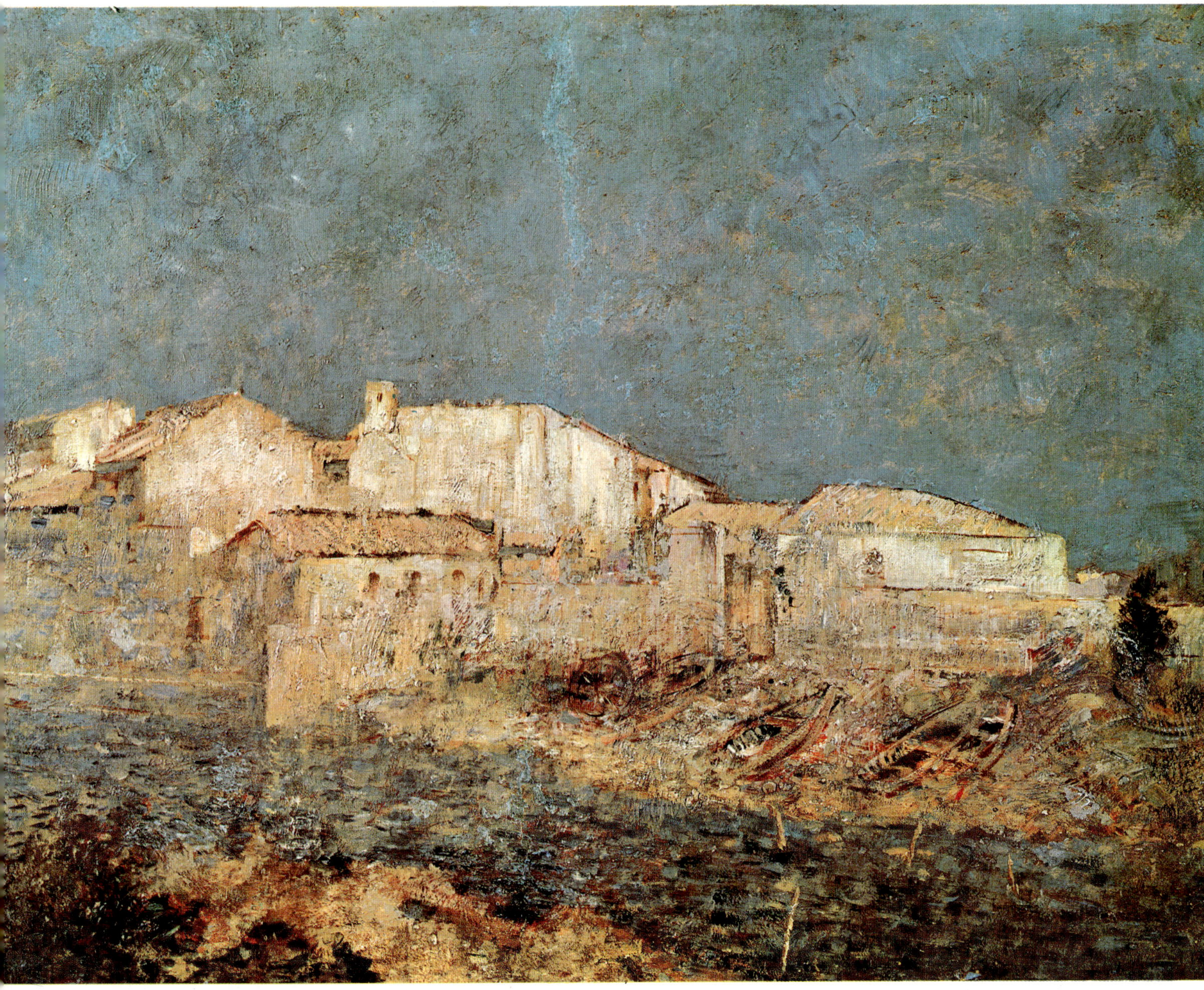

12. *View of Venice* - after 1908. Musée des Beaux-Arts, Bordeaux.

13. *The interior of the library at Fontfroide Abbey, near Montpellier.*

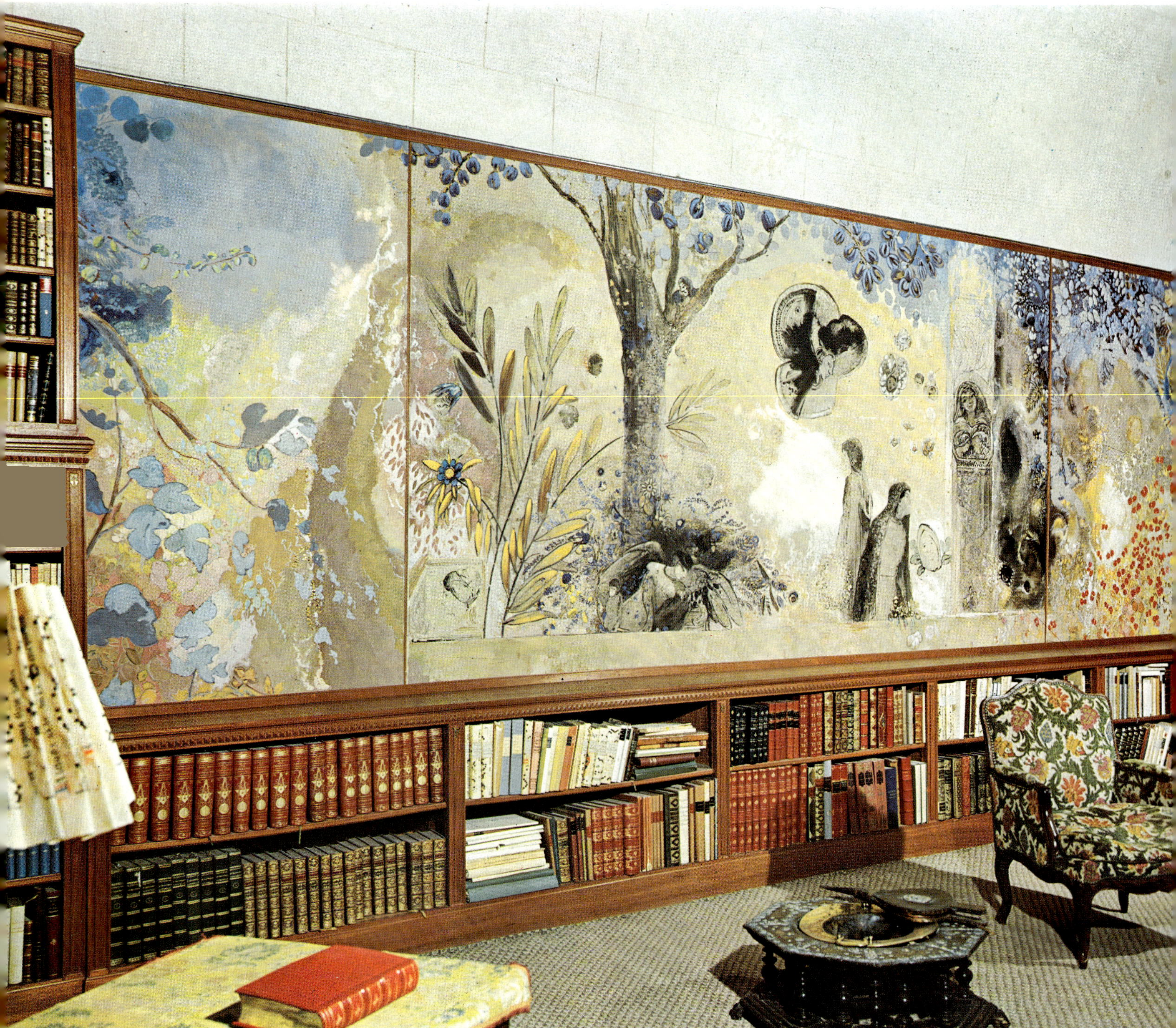

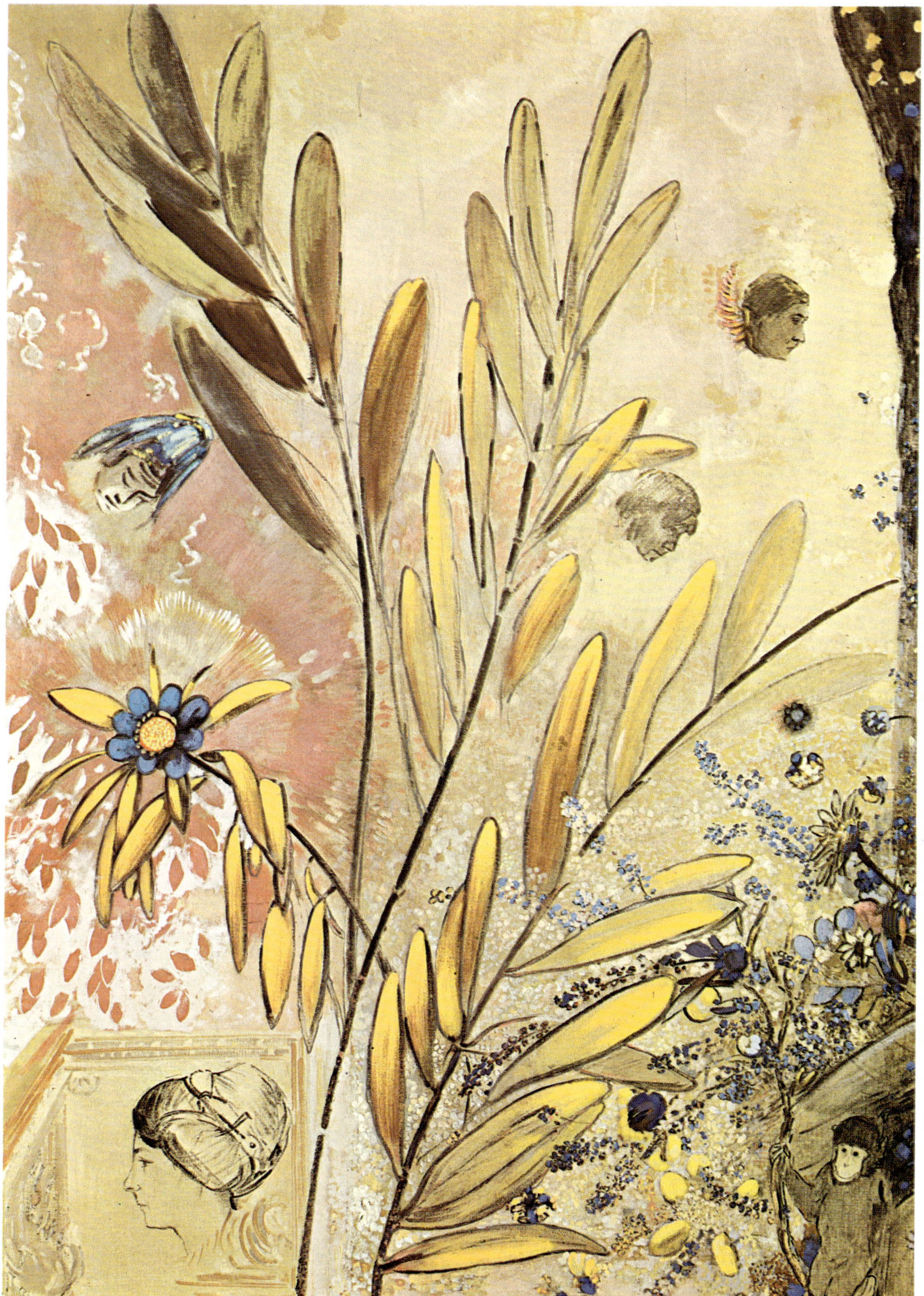

14. *Bas-relief: detail of the panel "Night"* - Library of Fontfroide Abbey.

15. *The Black Butterfly: detail of the panel "Night"* - Library of Fontfroide Abbey.

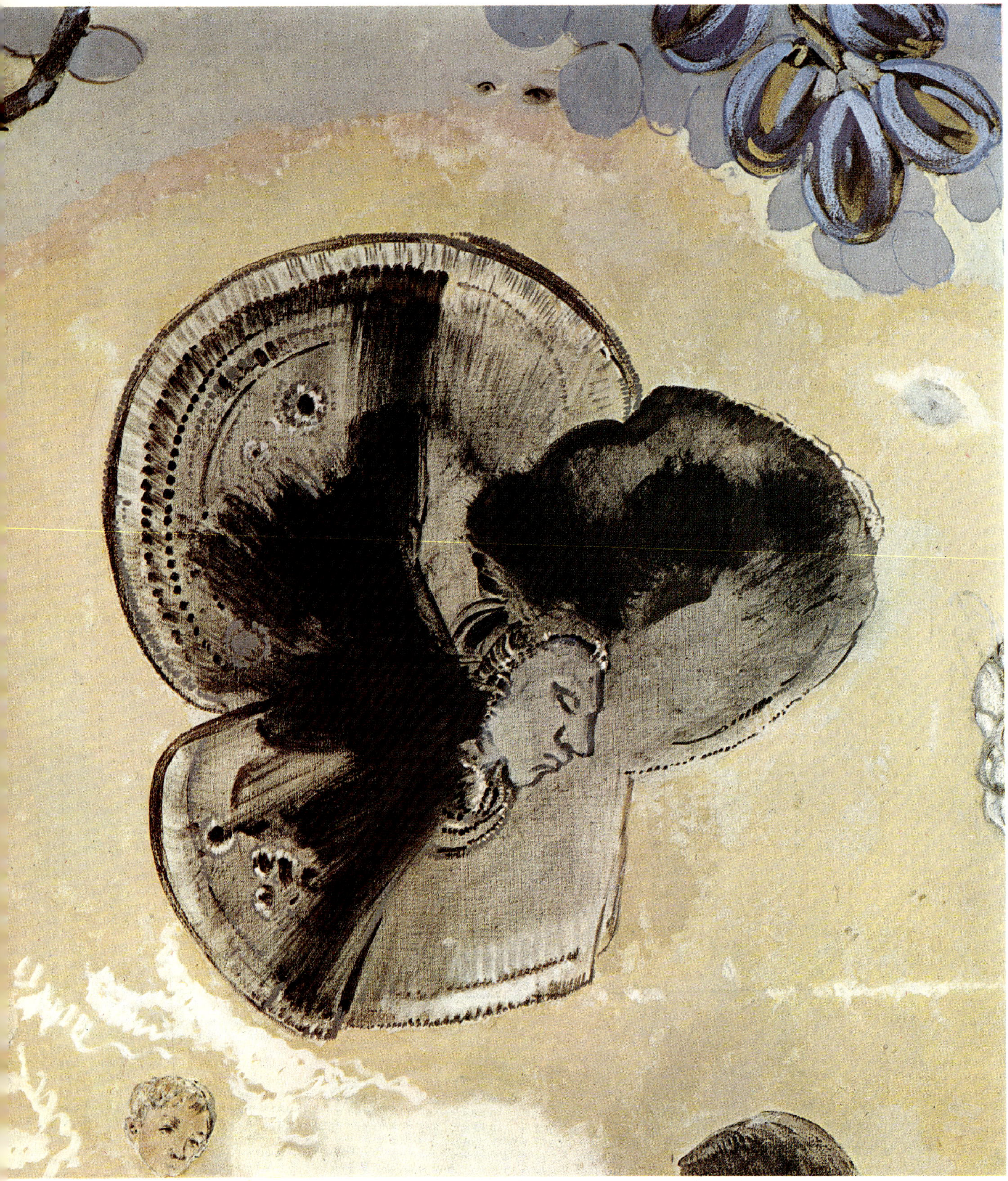

16. *Detail of the panel "Night"* - Library of Fontfroide Abbey.

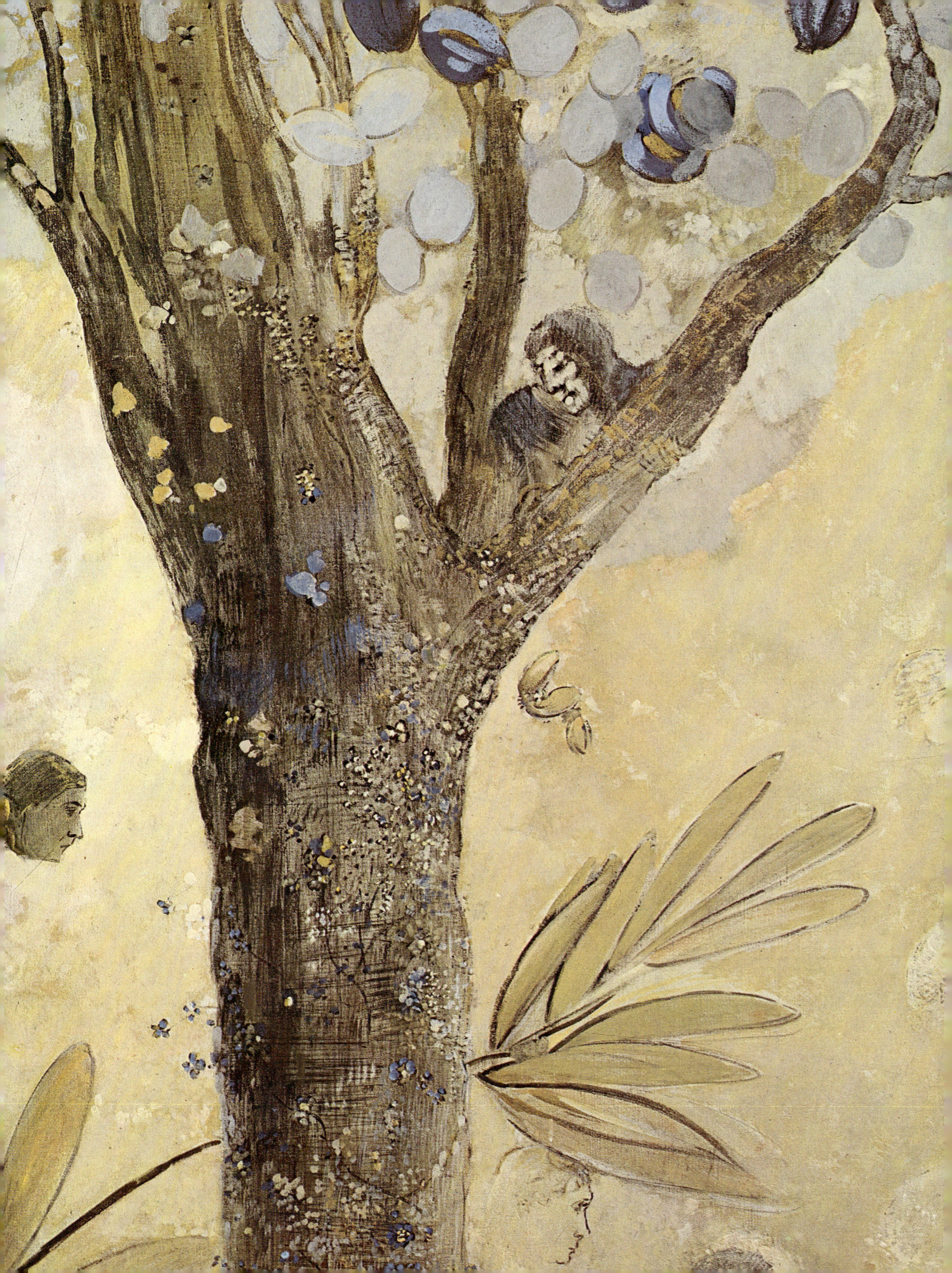

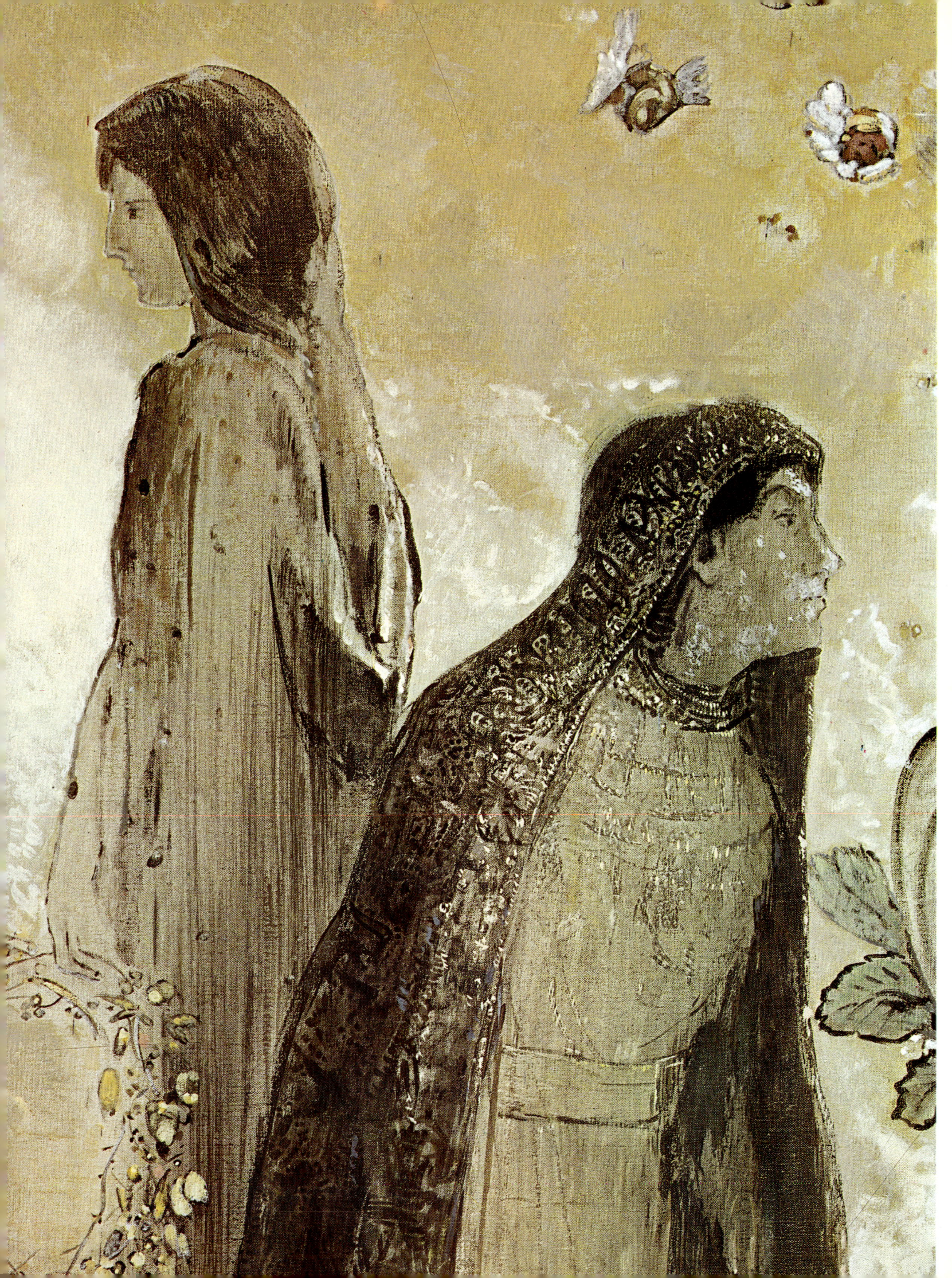

17. *Two Women in Mourning: detail of the panel "Night"* - Library of Fontfroide Abbey.

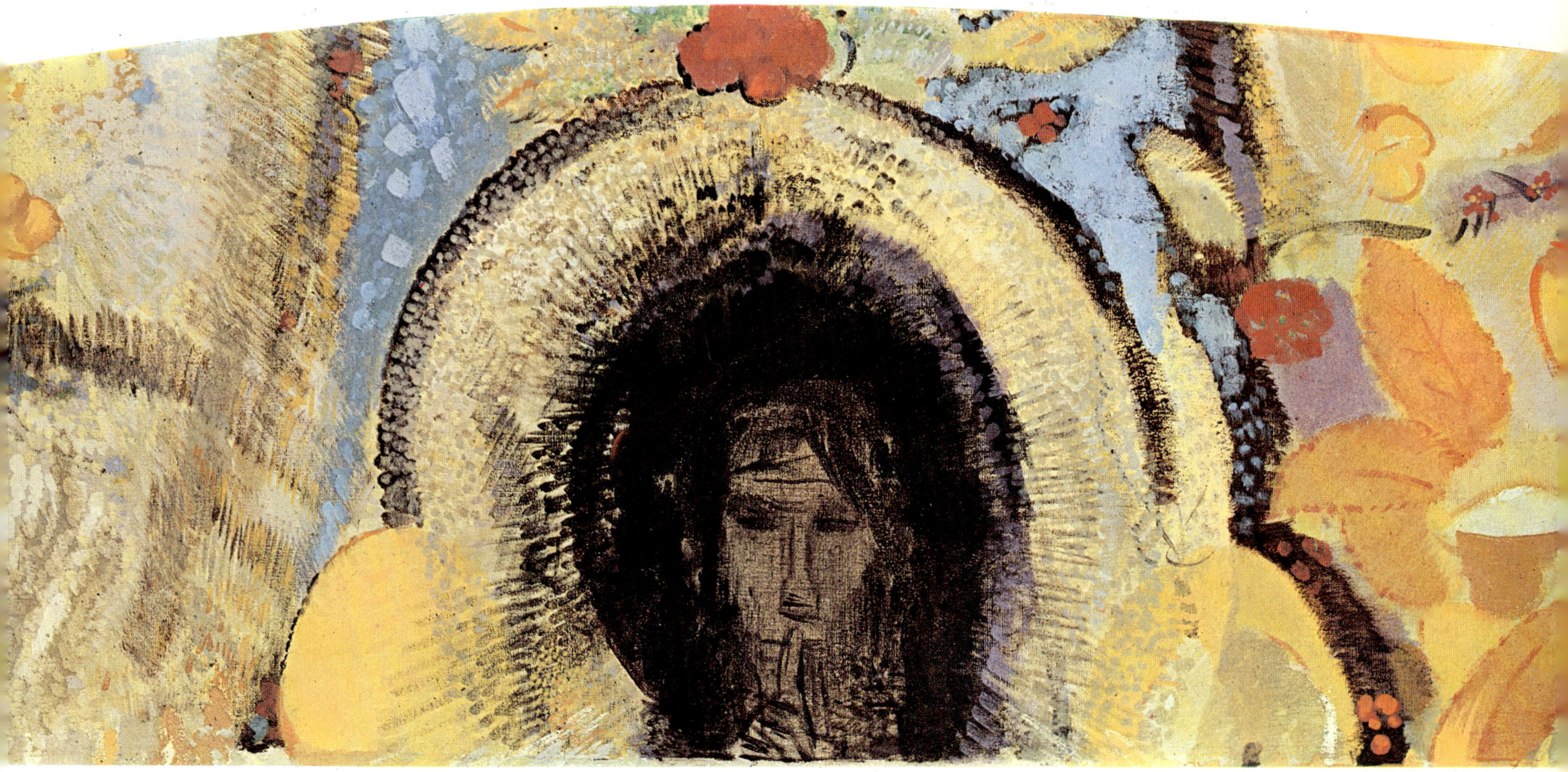

18. *Silence: detail of the panel beneath the main entrance* - Library of Fontfroide Abbey.

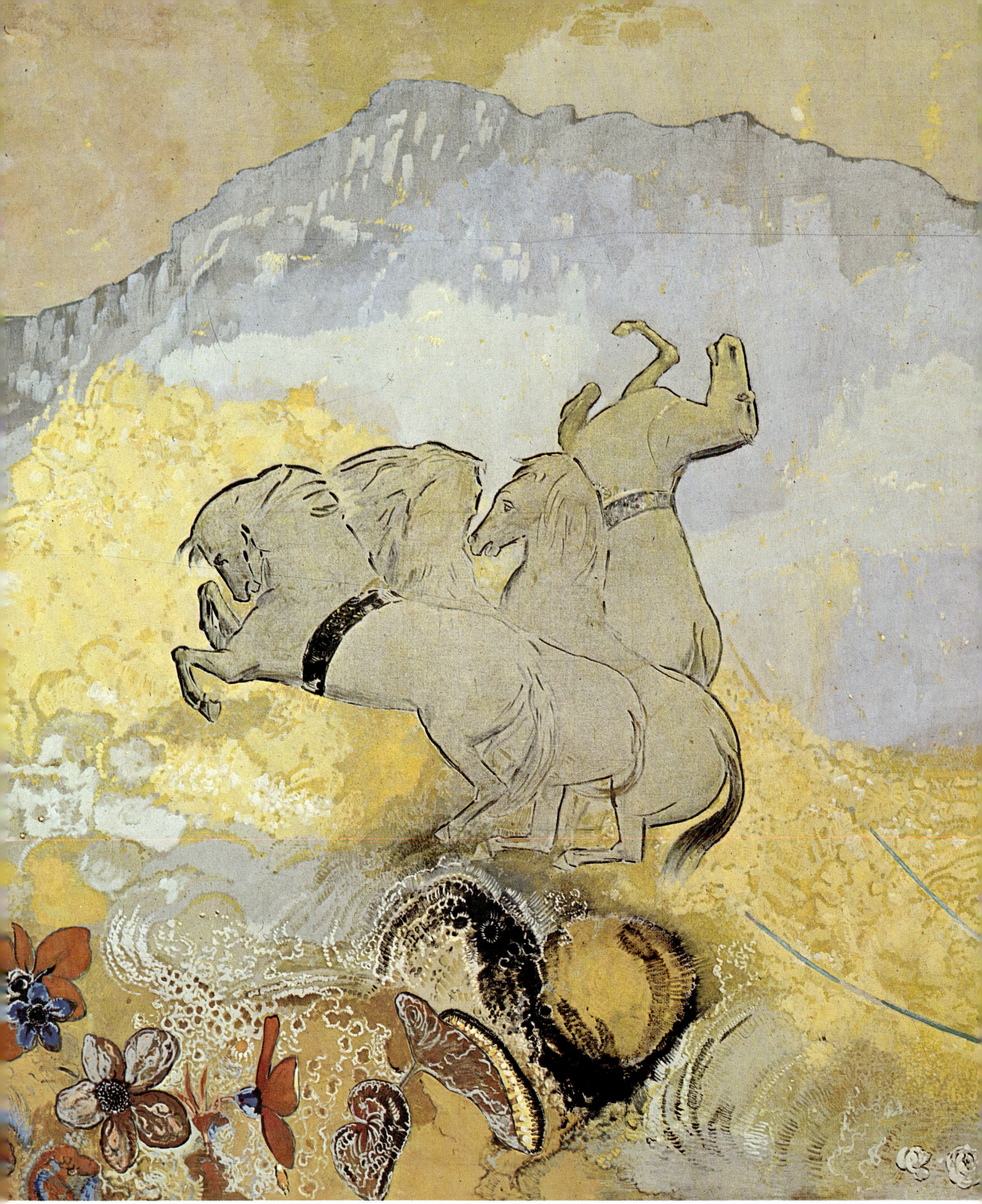

19. *Apollo's Sun Chariot: detail of the panel "Day" (central part)* - Library of Fontfroide Abbey.

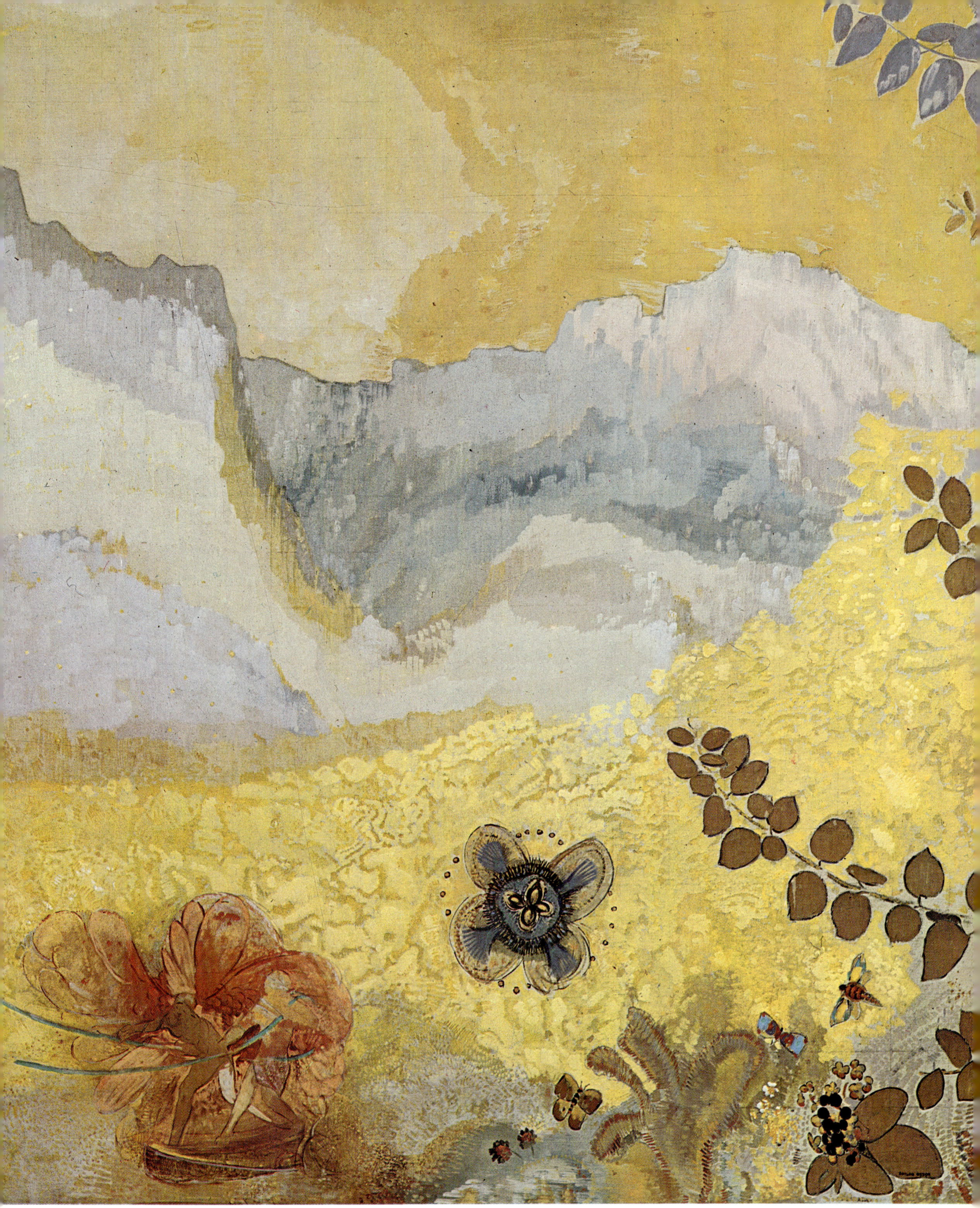

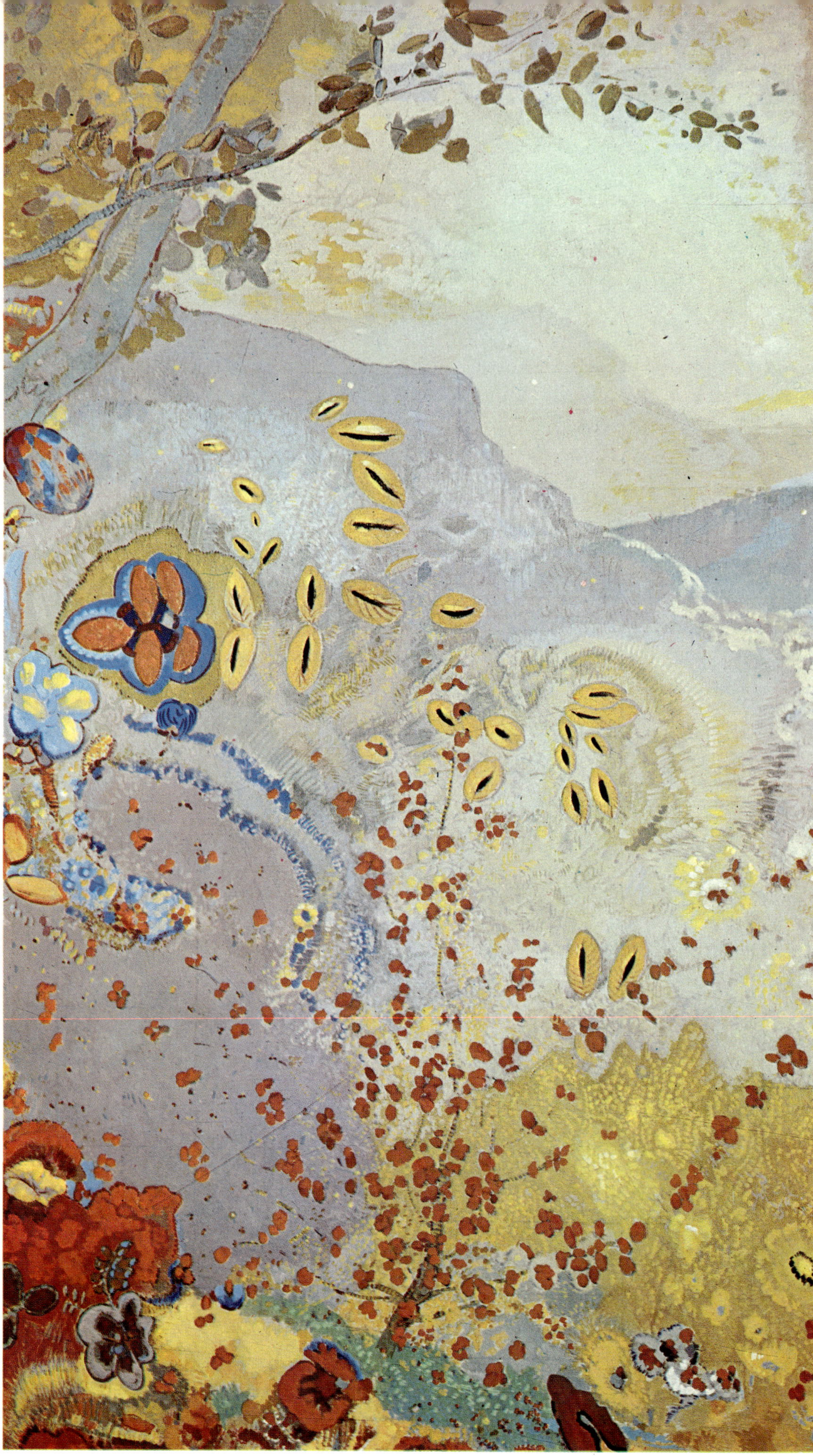

20. *Meanders: detail of the panel "Day" (left-hand side)* - Library of Fontfroide Abbey.

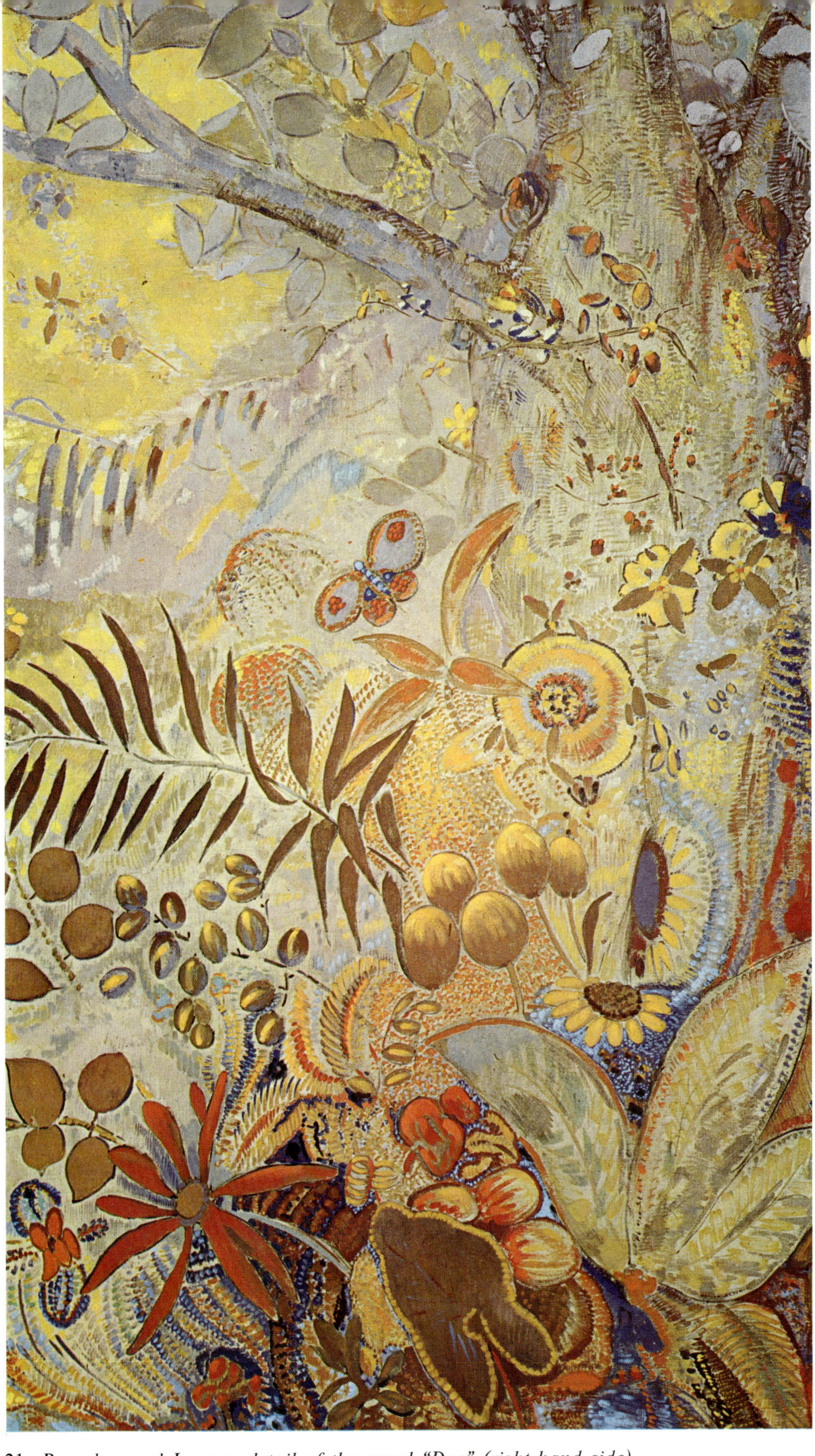

21. *Branches and Leaves: detail of the panel "Day" (right-hand side)* - Library of Fontfroide Abbey.

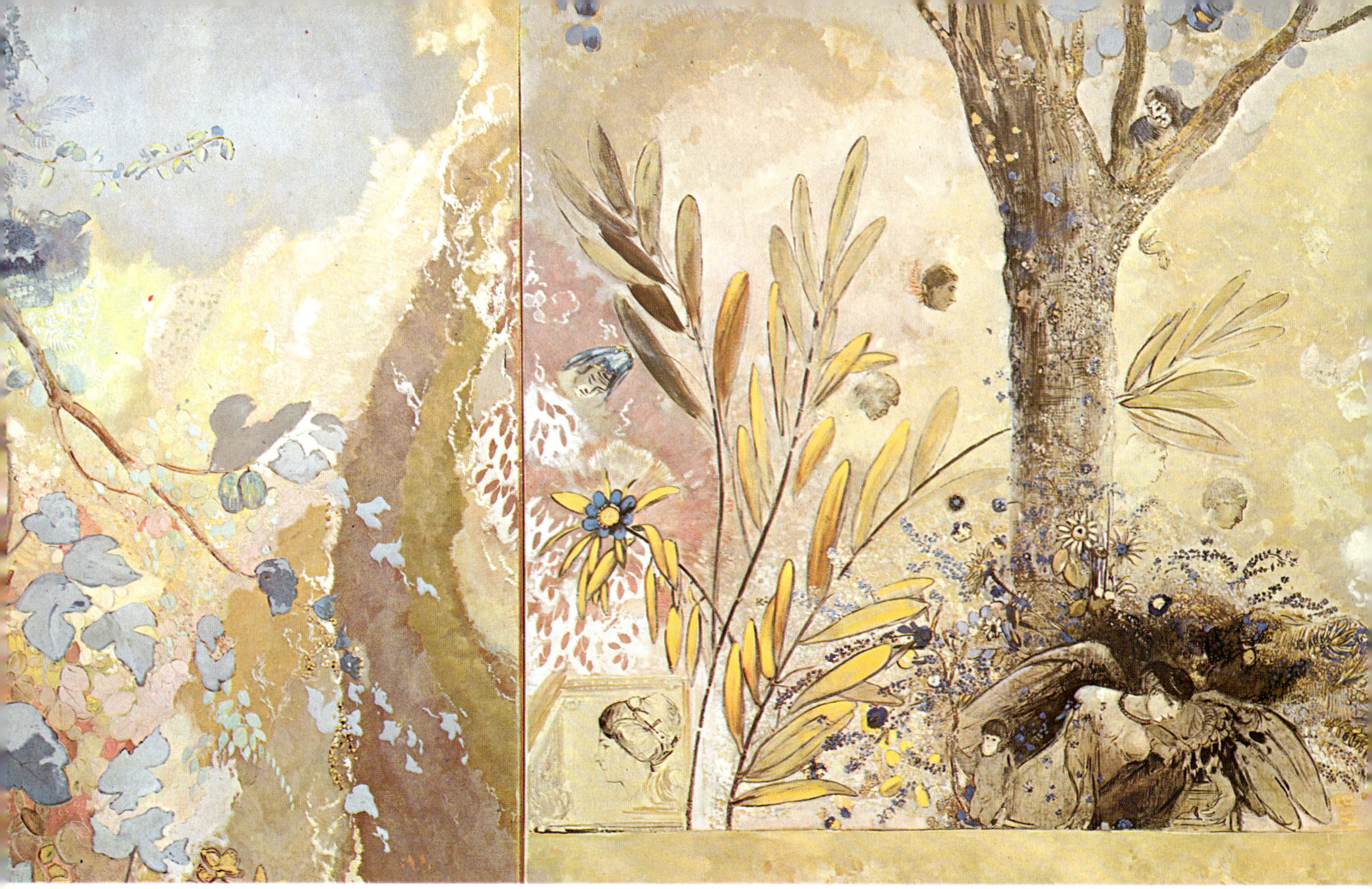

22. *The "Night" Panel* - 1910-11. Library of Fontfroide Abbey.

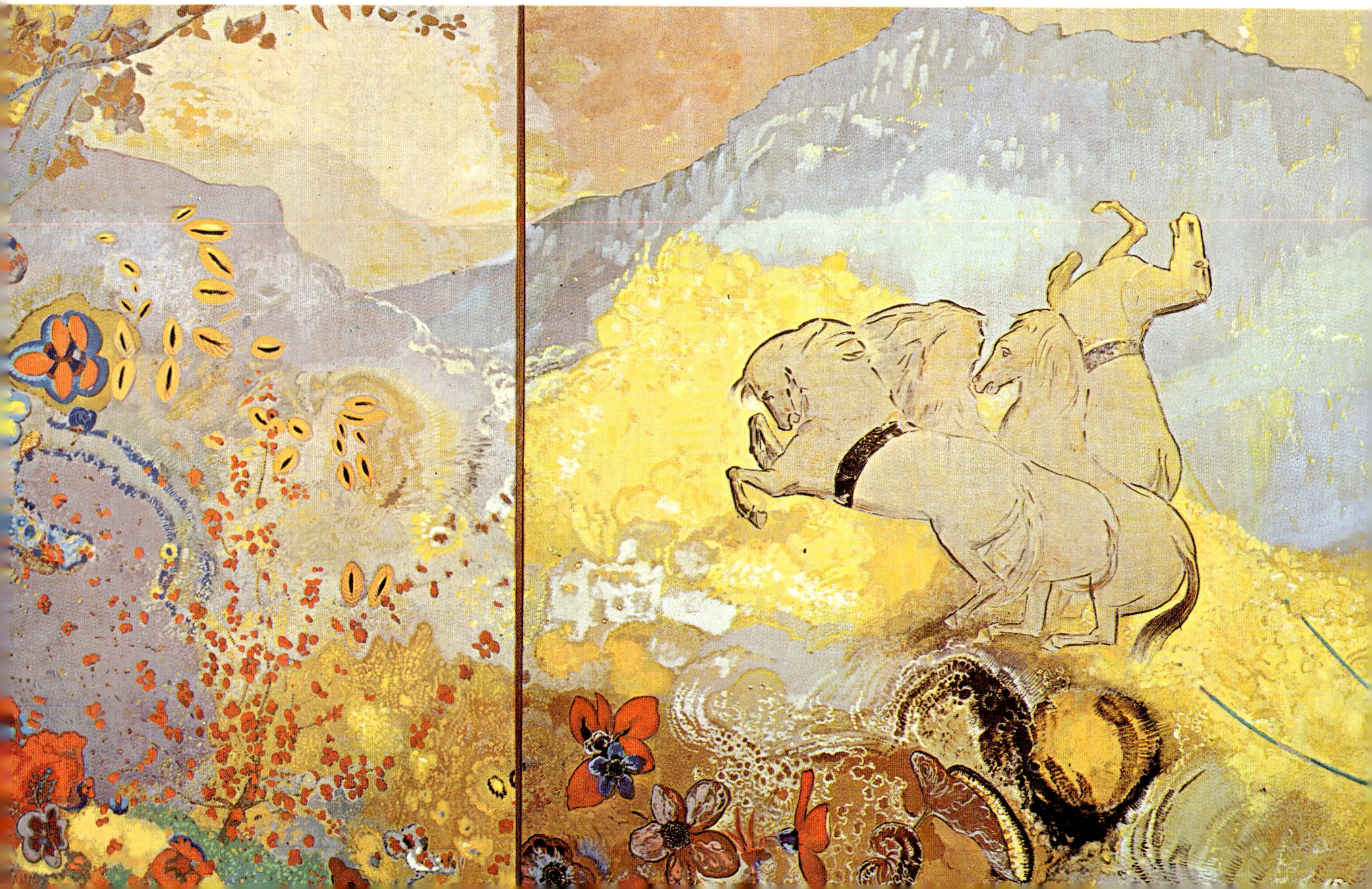

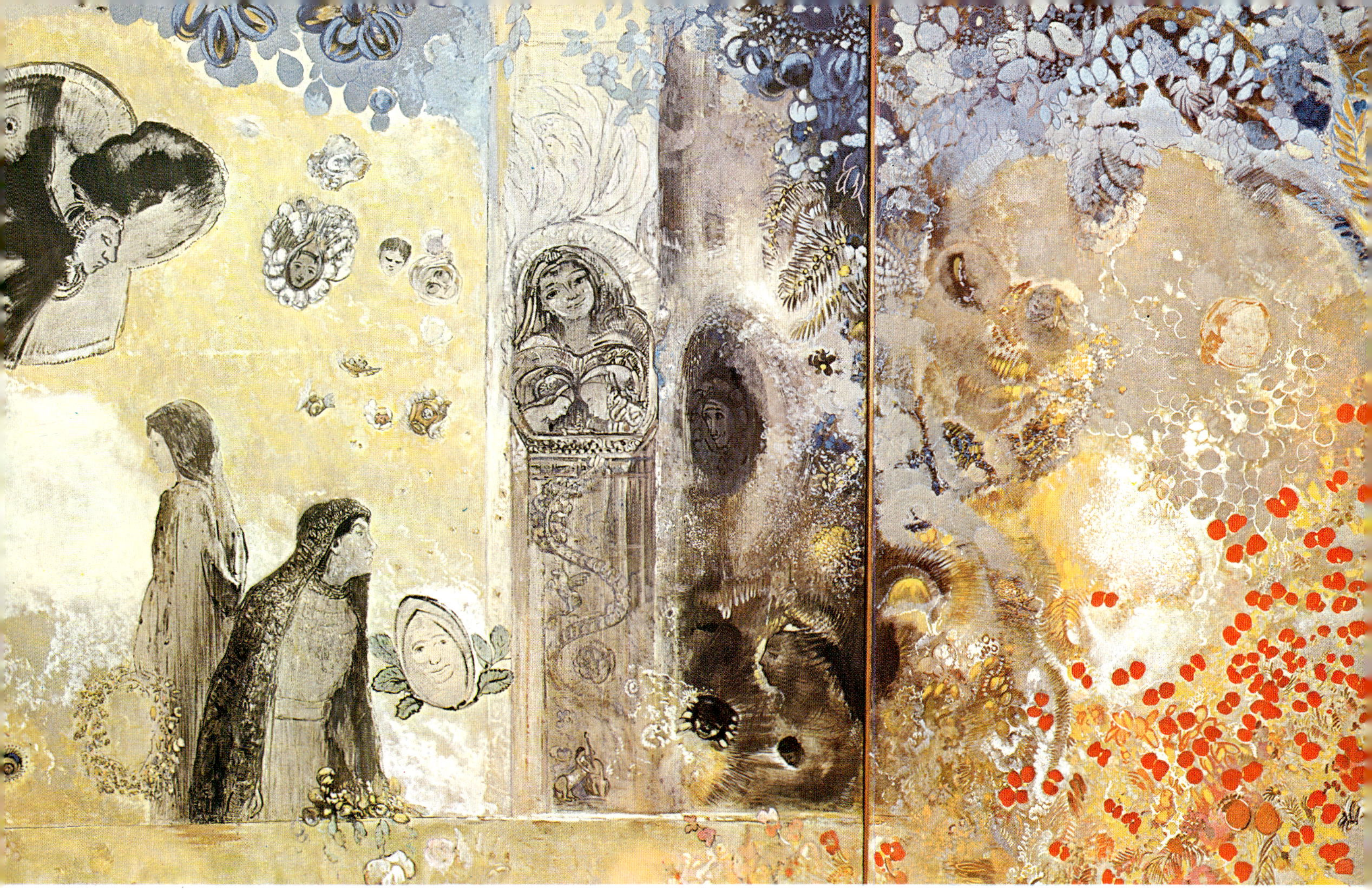

23. *The "Day" Panel* - 1910-11. Library of Fontfroide Abbey.

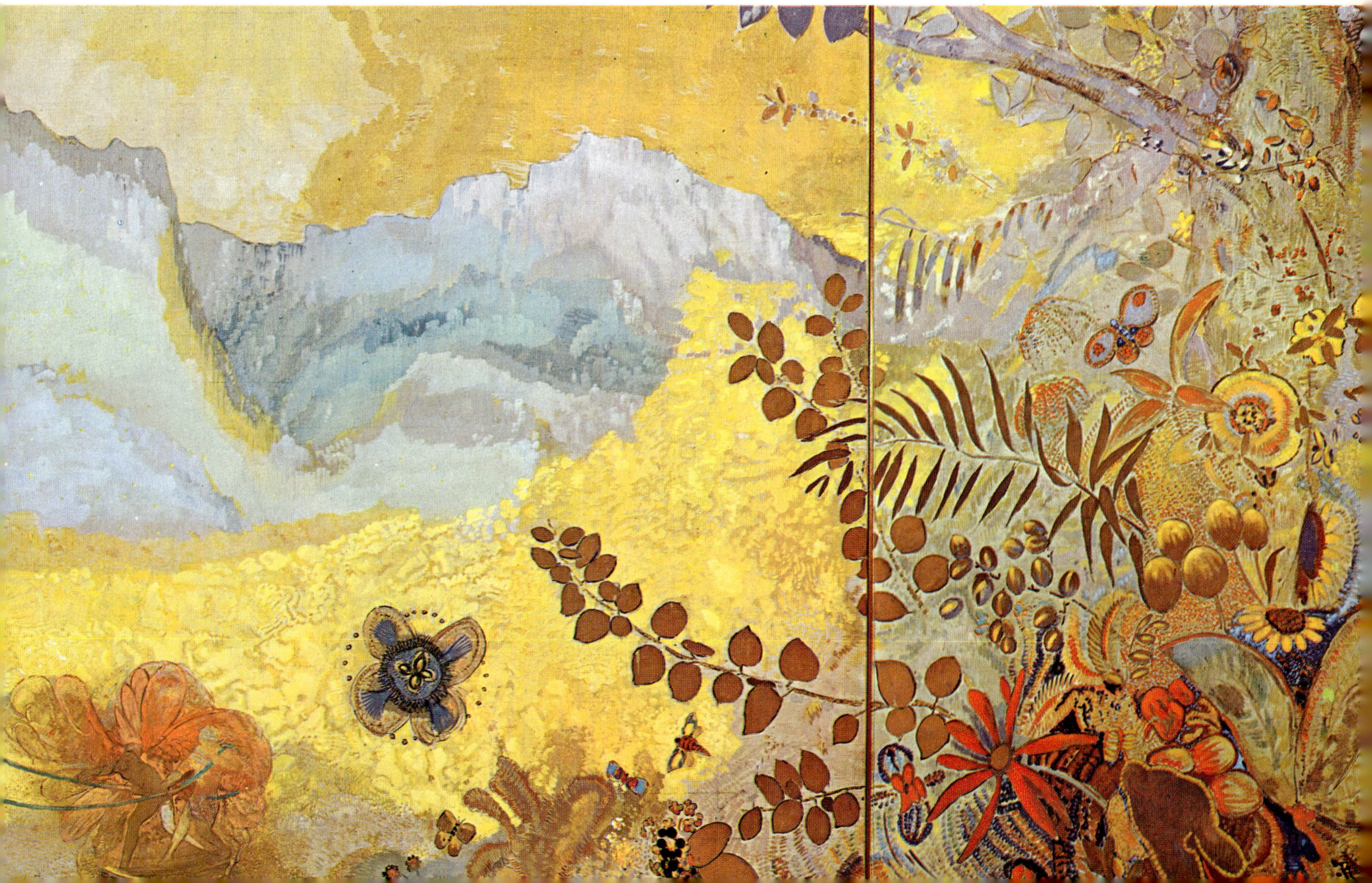

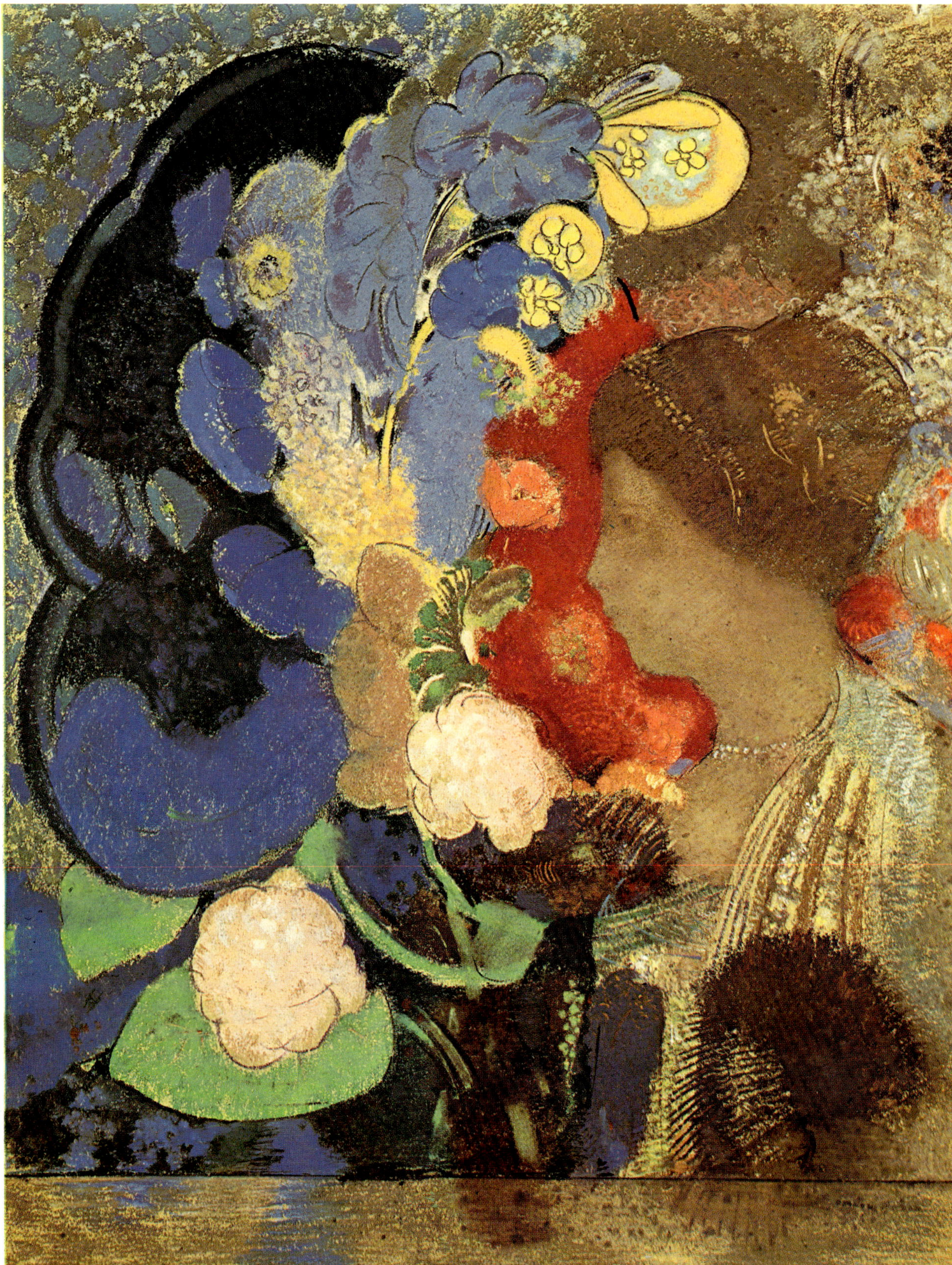

24. *Woman Amidst Flowers* - 1909-10. Jonas Collection, New York.

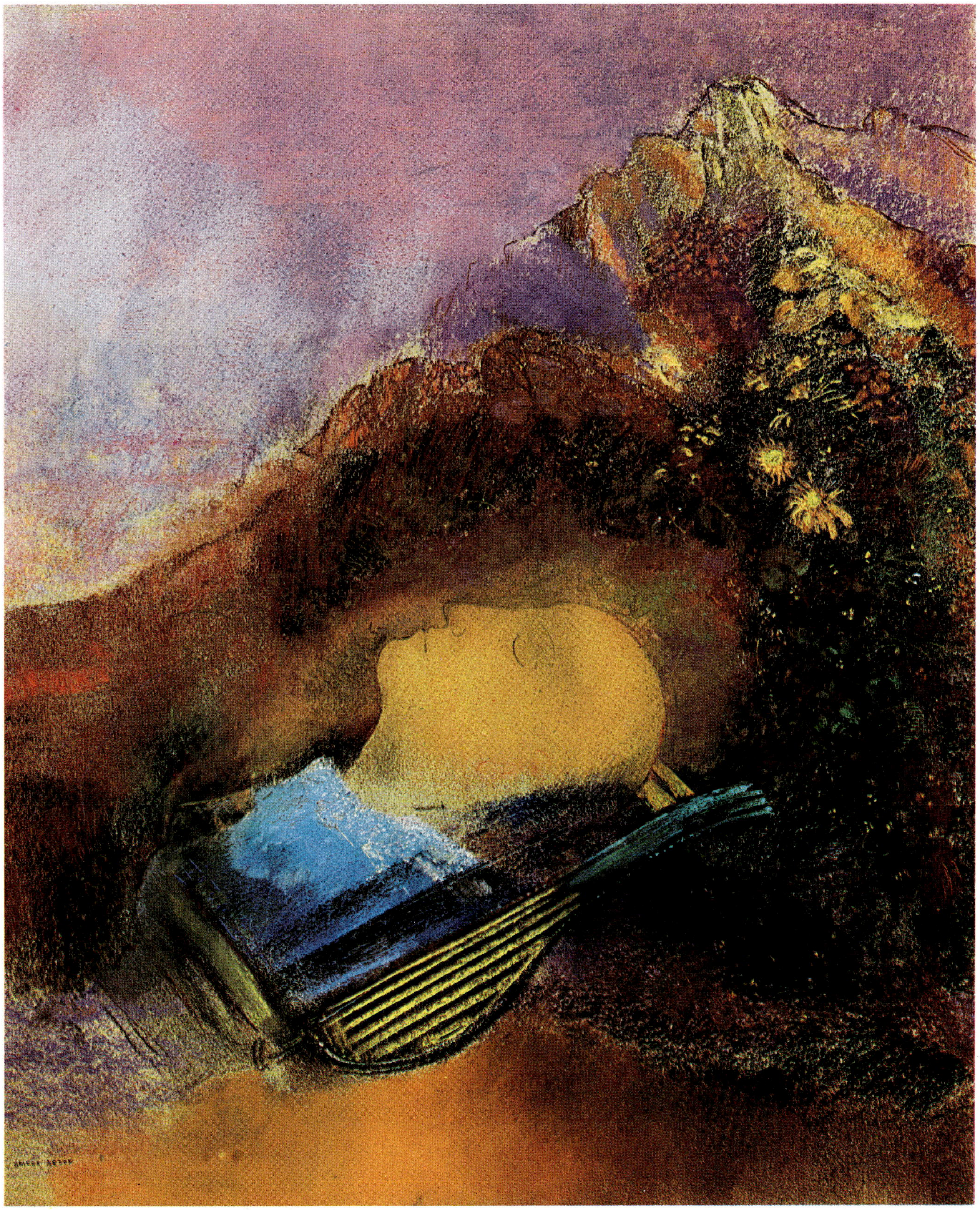

25. *Orpheus* - 1903 ca. Museum of Art, Cleveland.

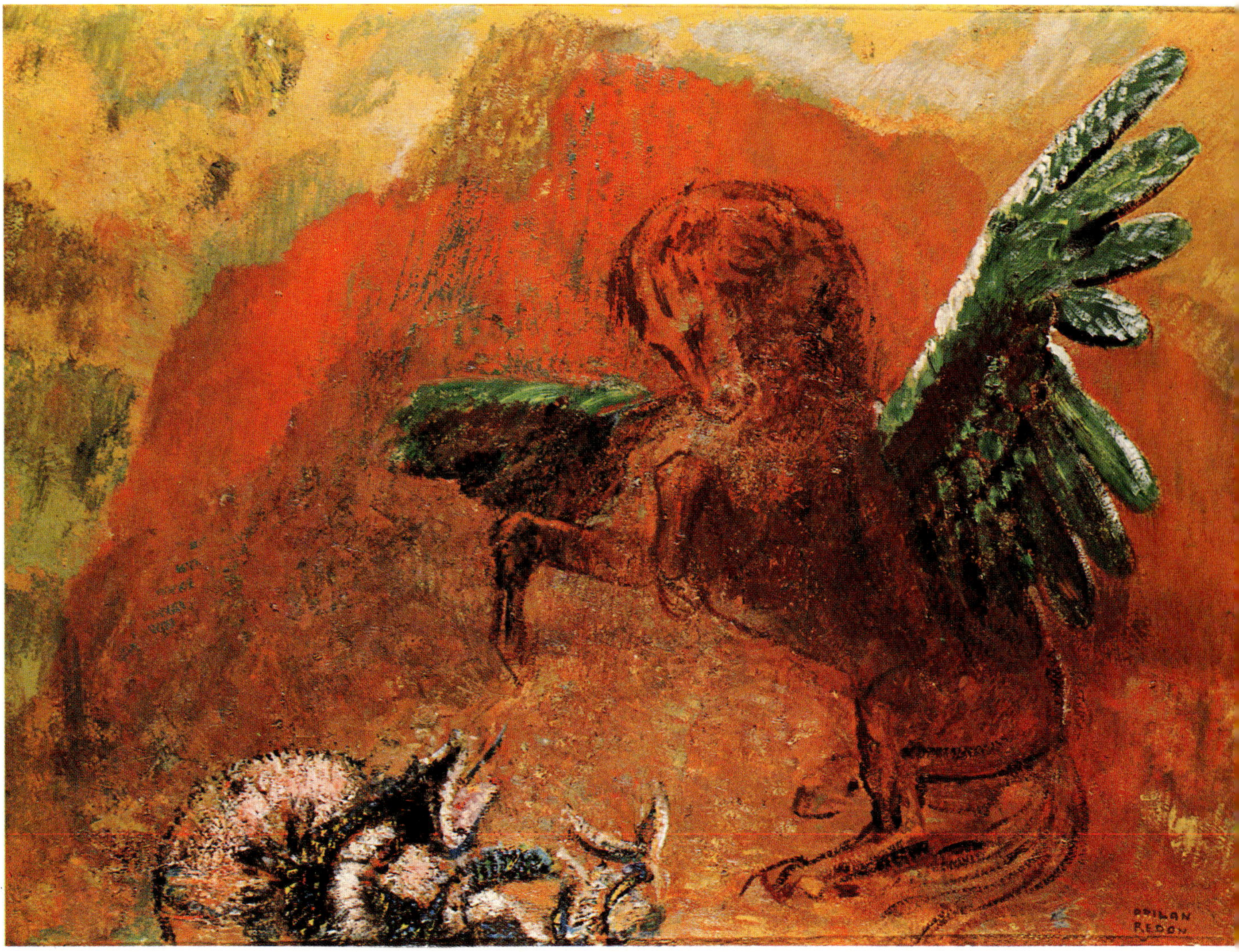

26. *Pegasus and the Dragon* - 1907 ca. Rijksmuseum Kröller-Müller, Otterlo.

27. *Cyclops* - 1895-1900. Rijksmuseum Kröller-Müller, Otterlo.

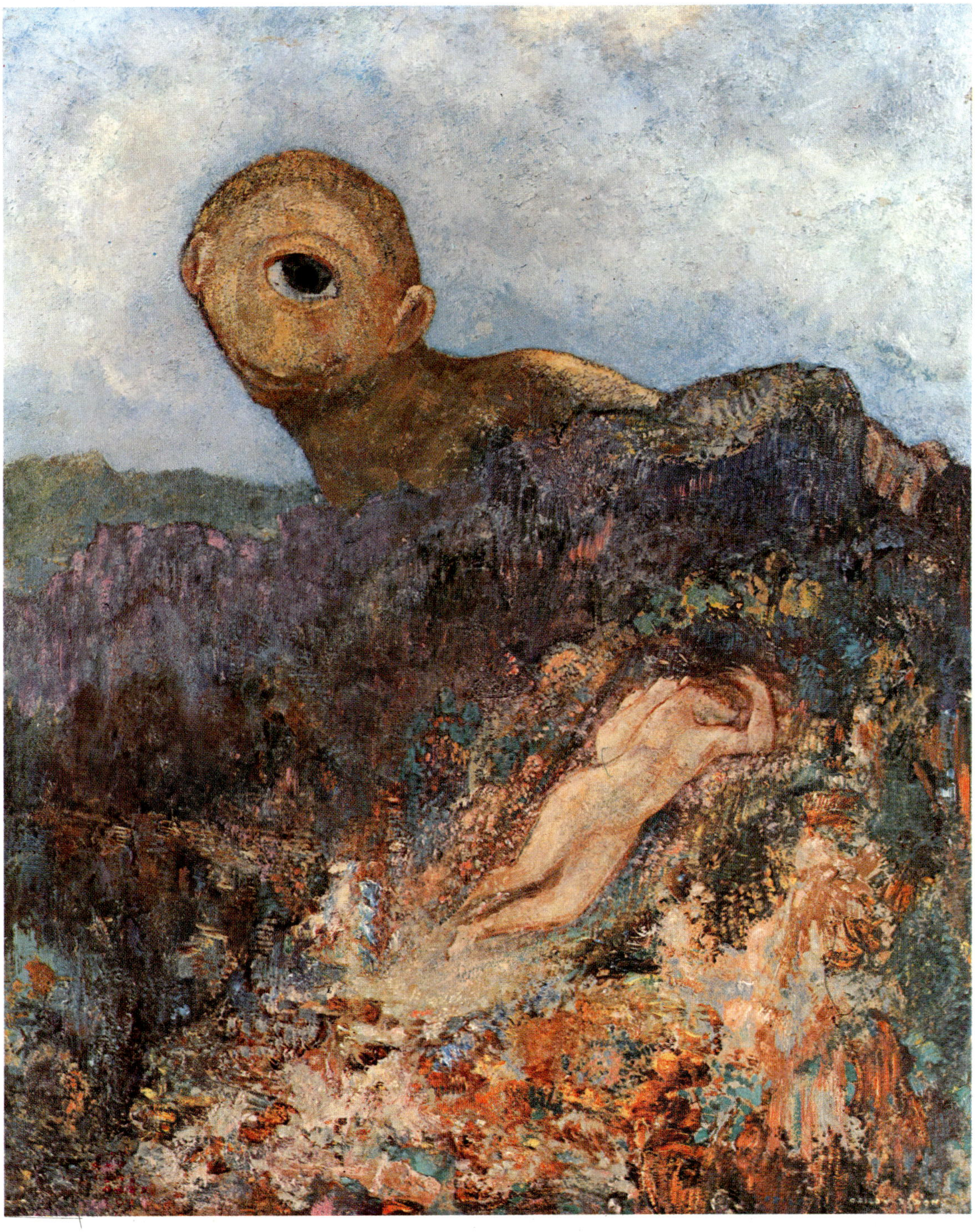

28. *Roger and Angelica* - 1900 ca.
The Museum of Modern Art, Lillie P. Bliss Collection. New York.

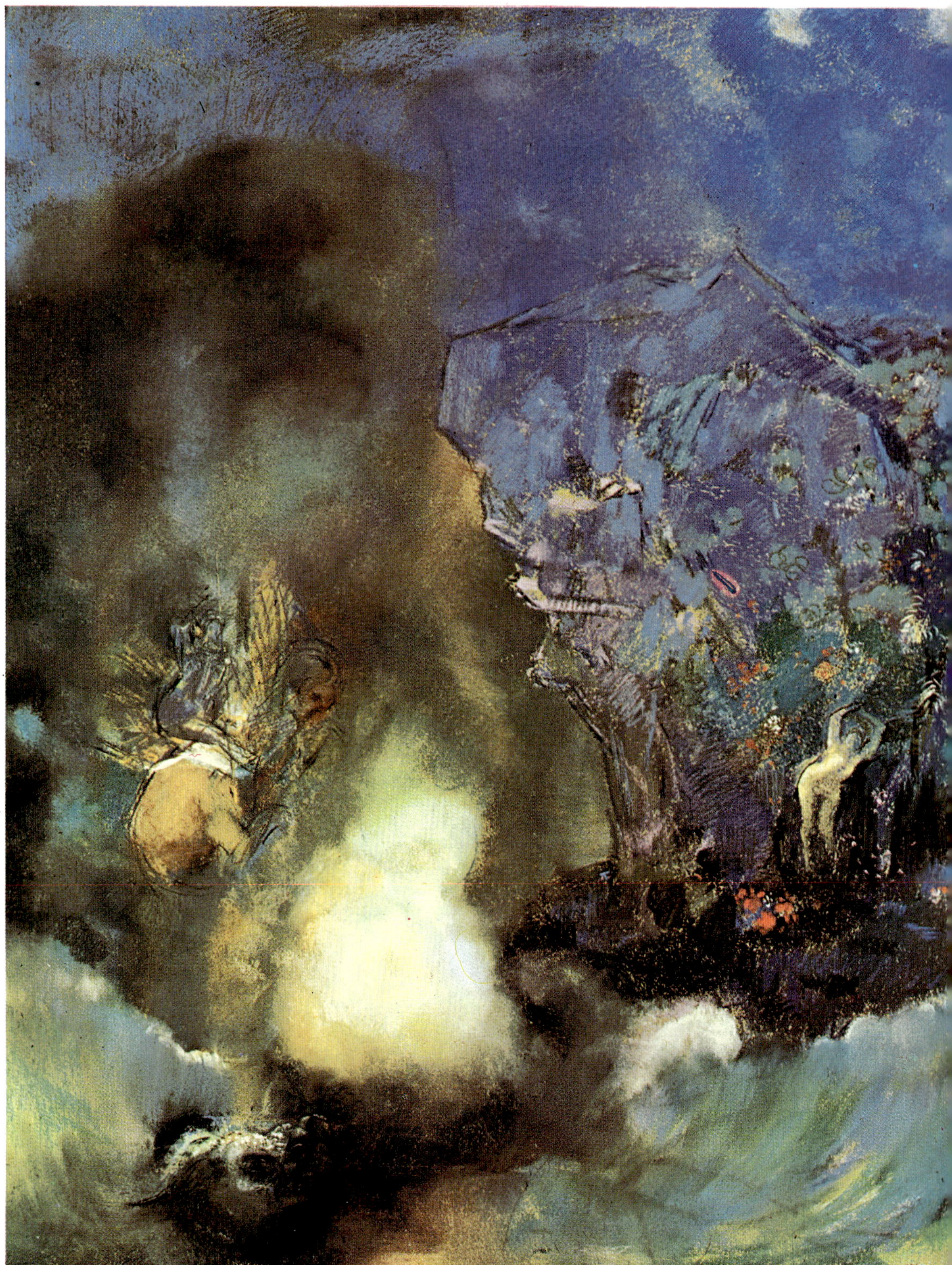

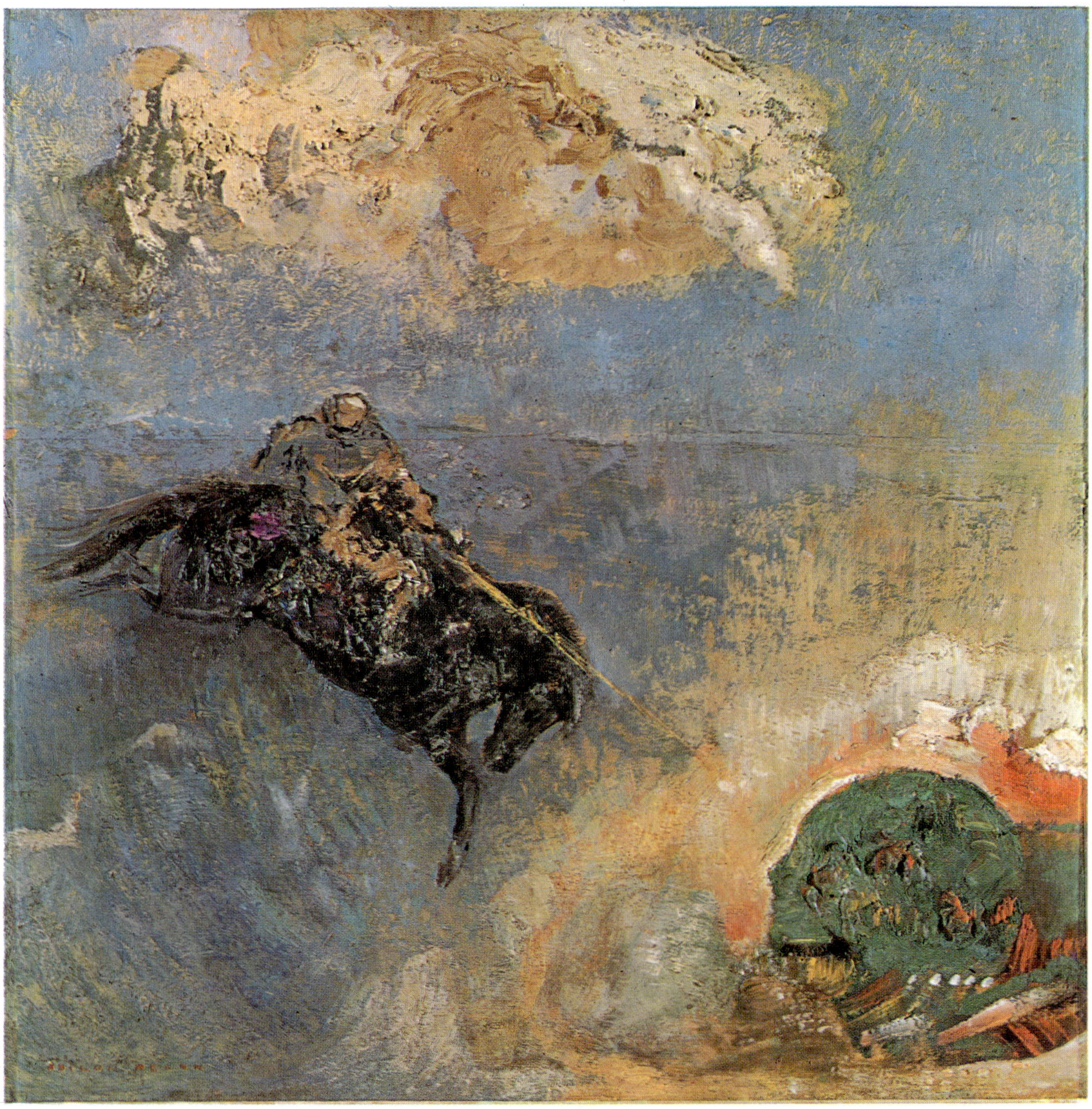

29. *Roger and Angelica* - 1909-1910. Rijksmuseum Kröller-Müller, Otterlo.

30. *Silence (a variation on the decoration at Fontfroide Abbey)* - 1911.
The Museum of Modern Art, New York.

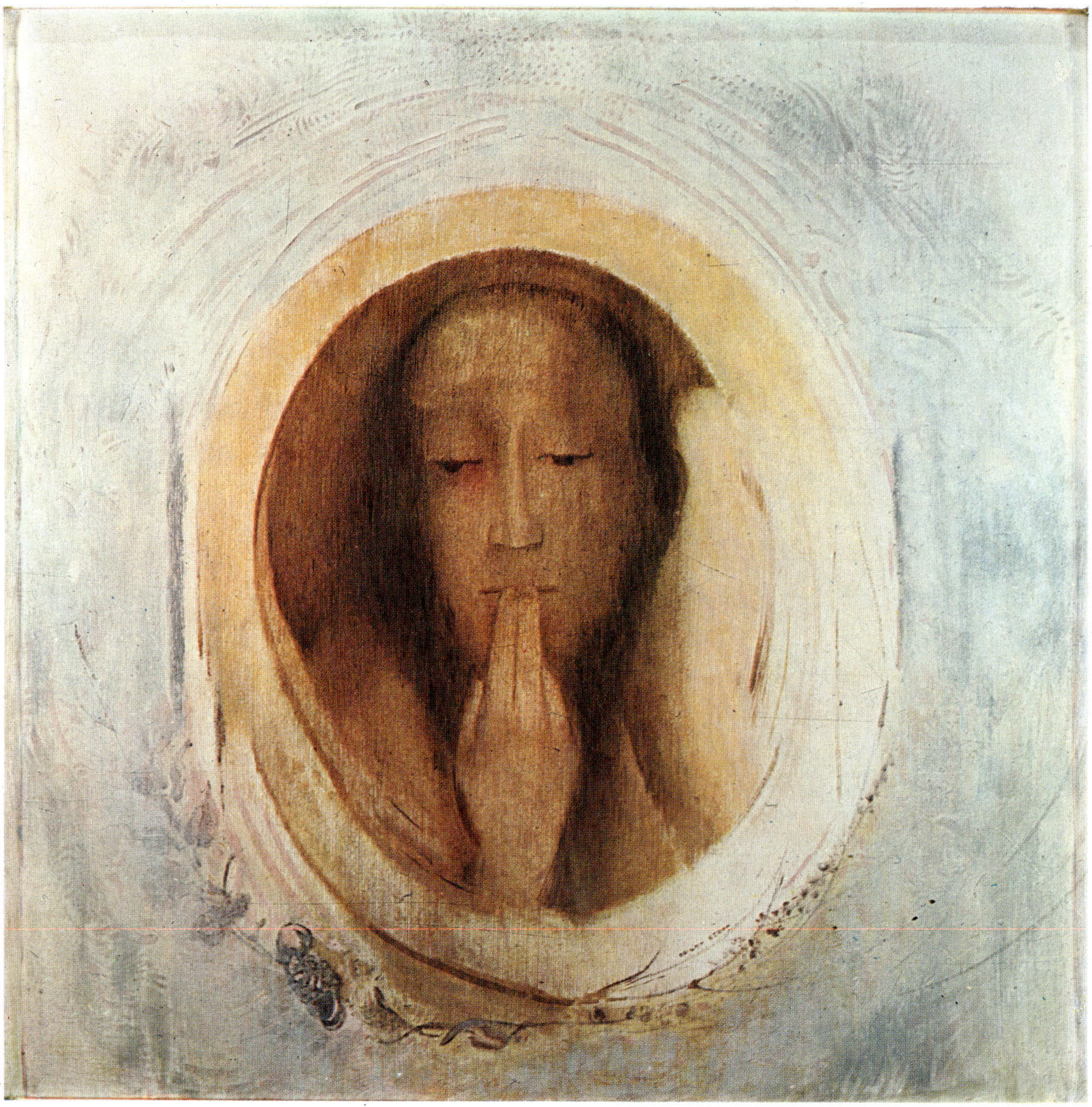

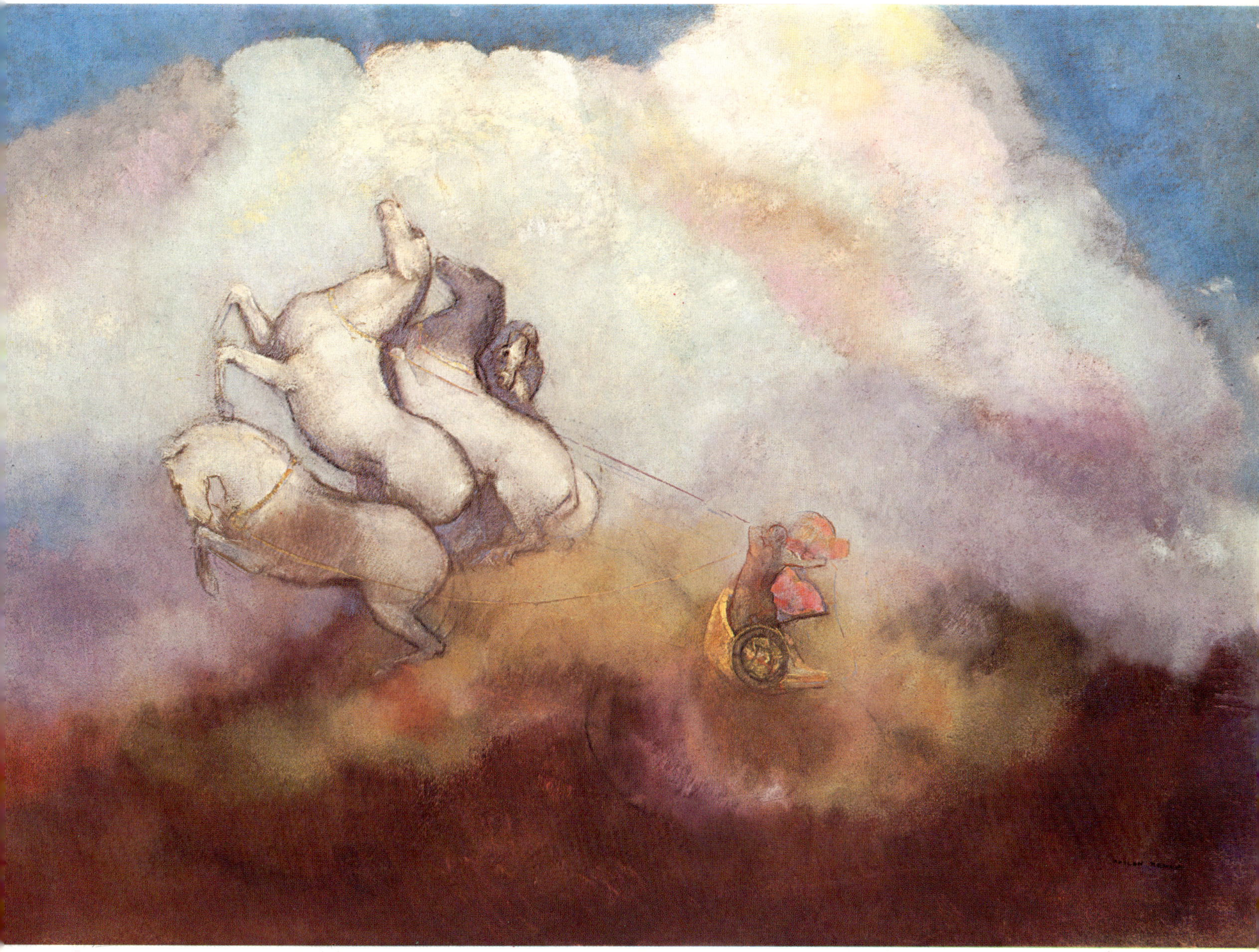

31. *Phaeton's Fall* - 1910 ca. Private collection, France.

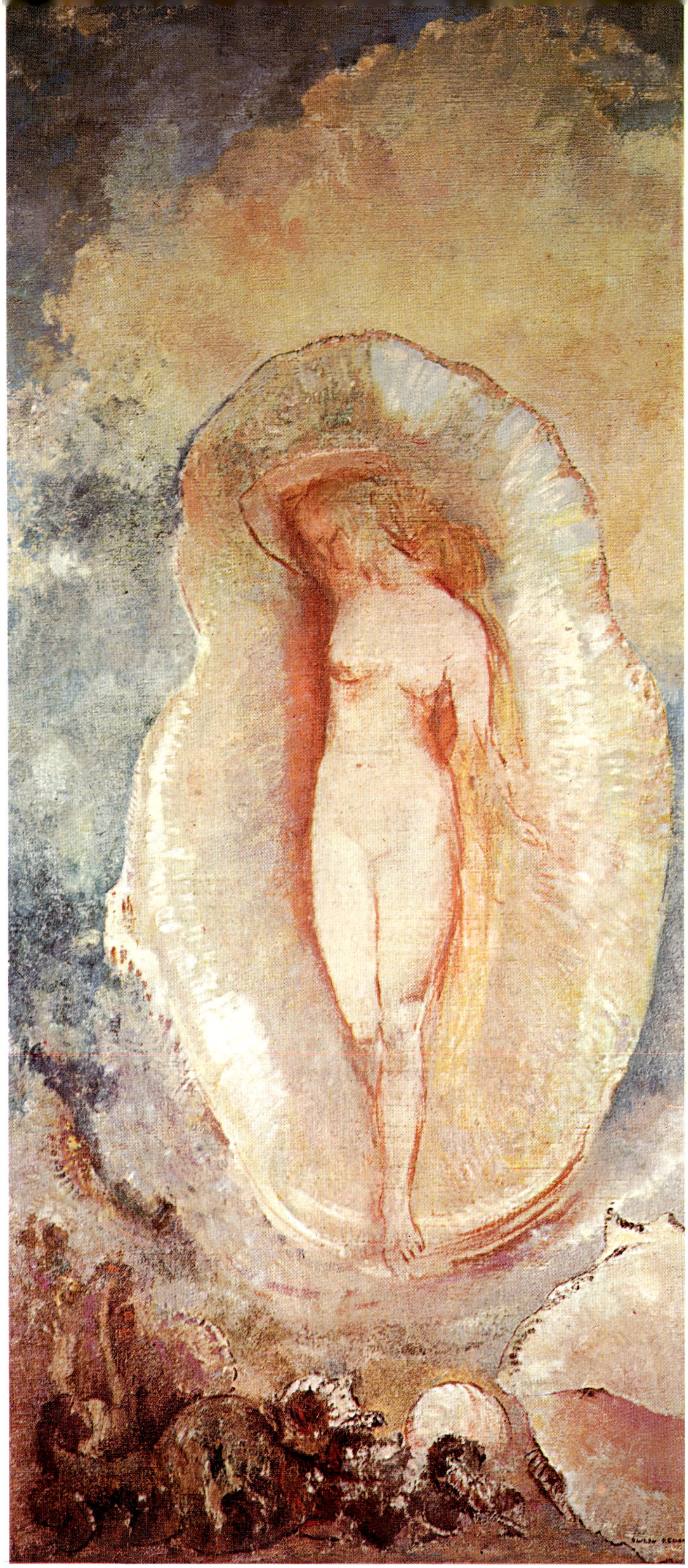

32. *The Birth of Venus* - 1912.
Stephen Higgons collection, Paris.

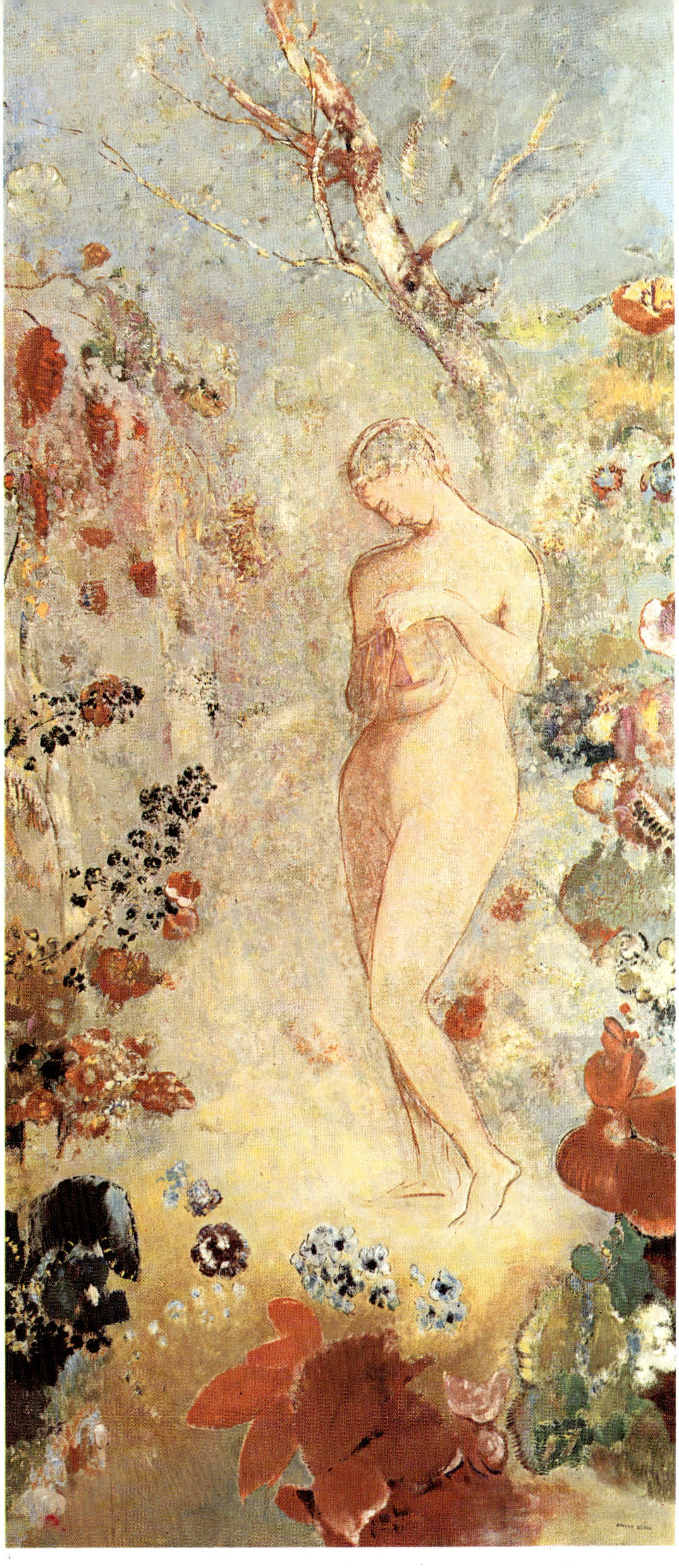

33. *Pandora* - 1910.
The Metropolitan Museum of Art,
Alexander M. Bing legacy. New York.

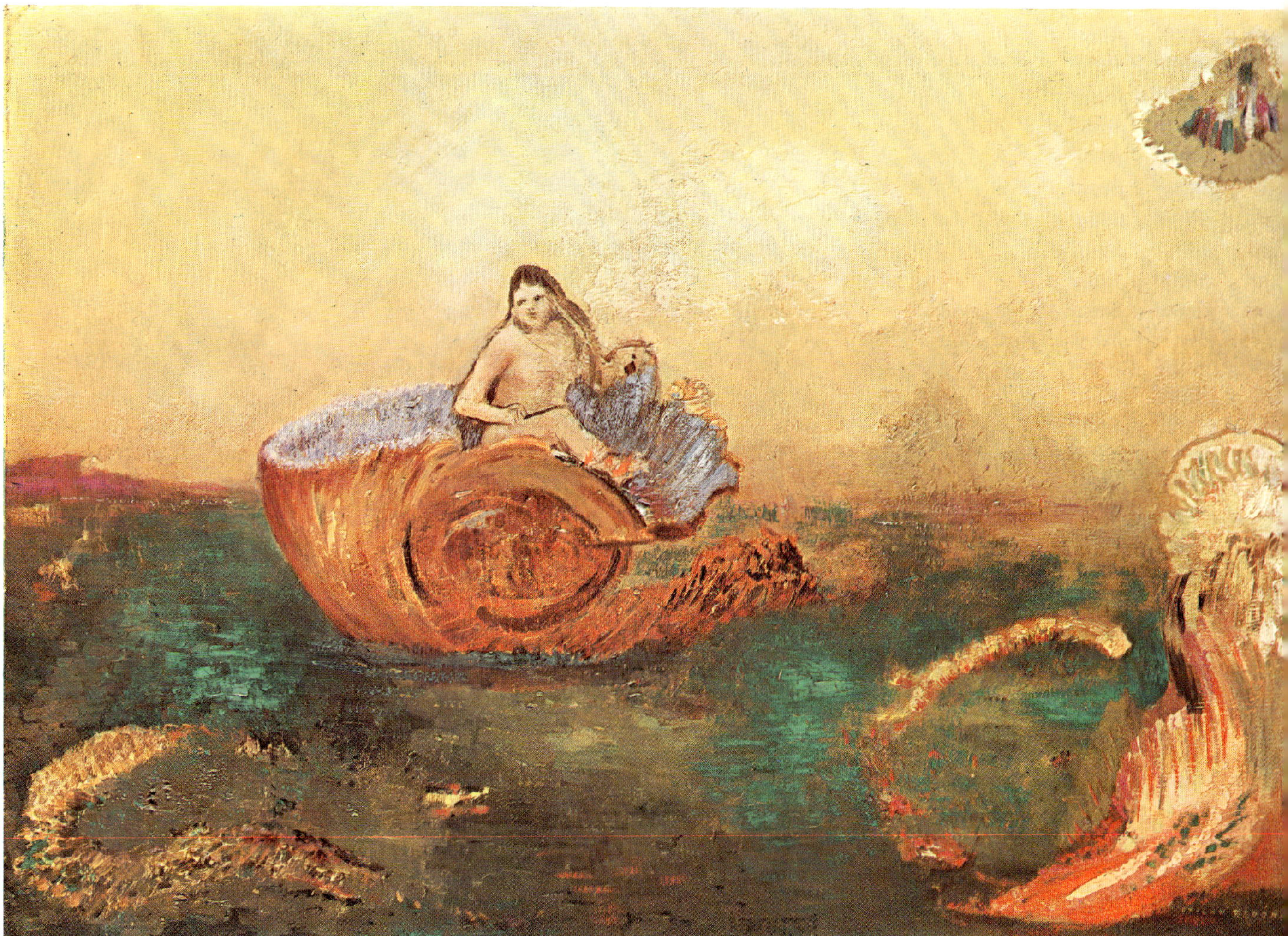

34. *The Birth of Venus* - 1902. Private collection, USA.

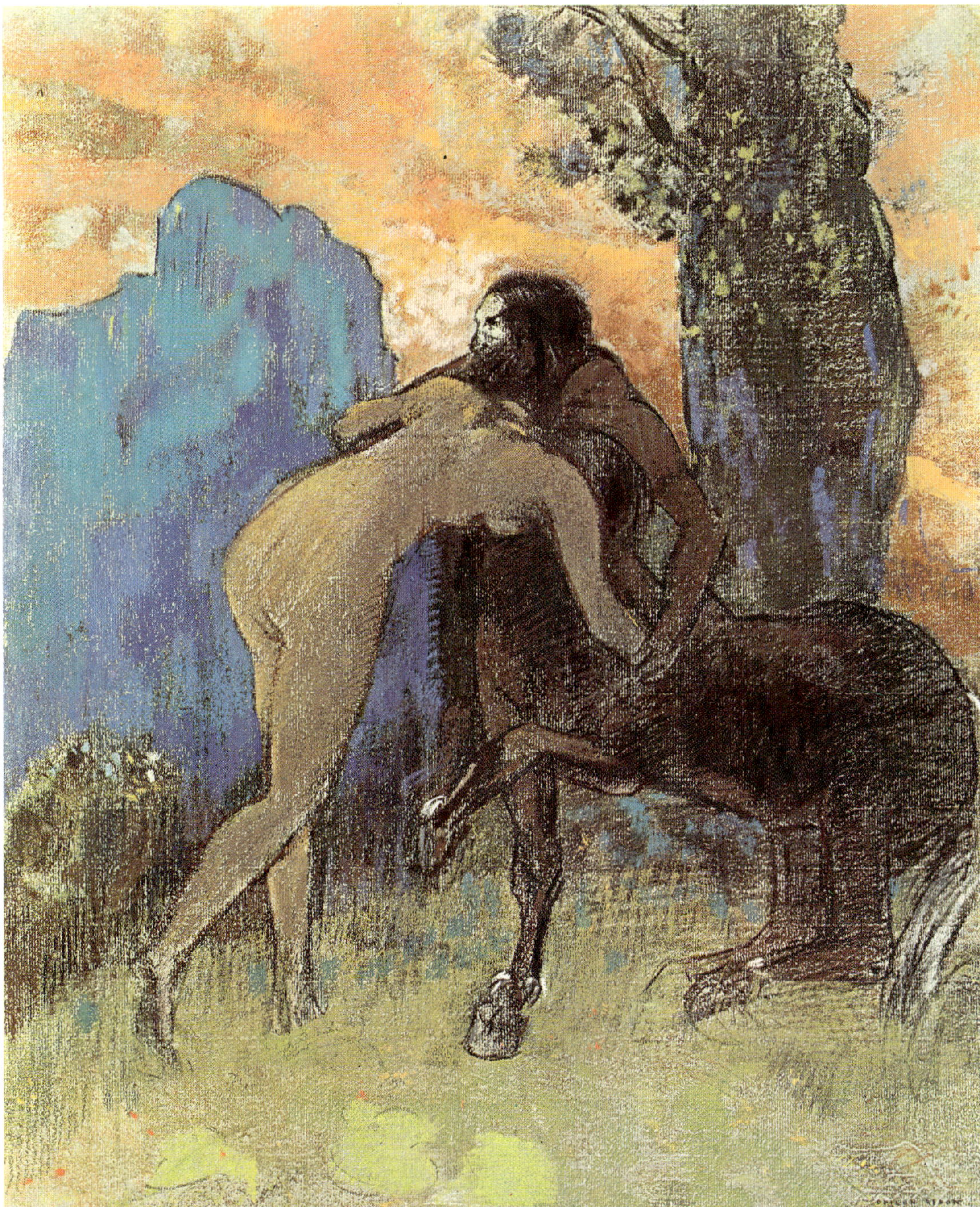

35. *Woman and Centaur* - 1900-1910. Private collection, France.

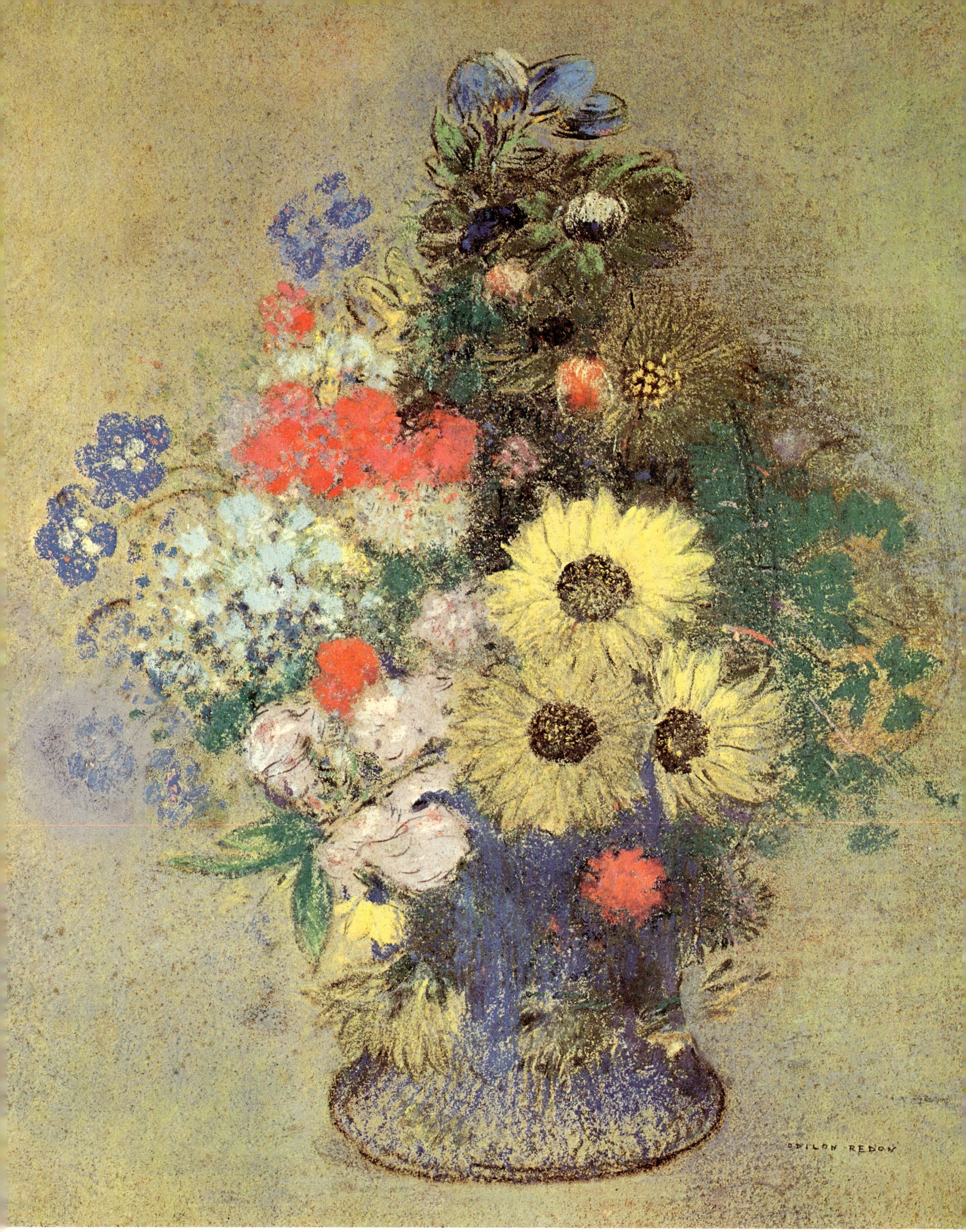
ODILON REDON

36. *Vase of Flowers* - Private collection, USA.

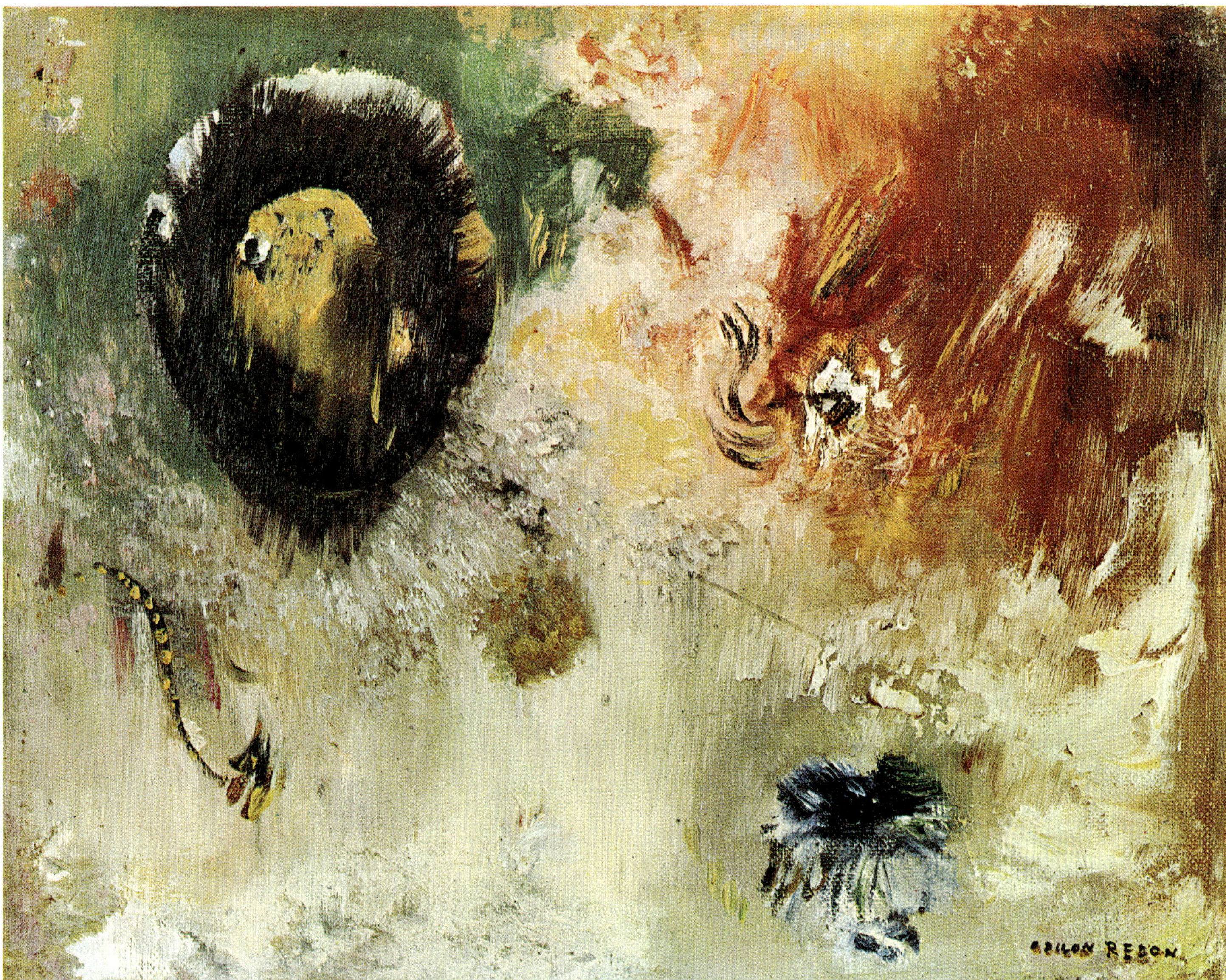

37. *Phantasmagoria* - Musée des Beaux-Arts, Bordeaux.

38. *Vase of Flowers* - Private collection, USA.

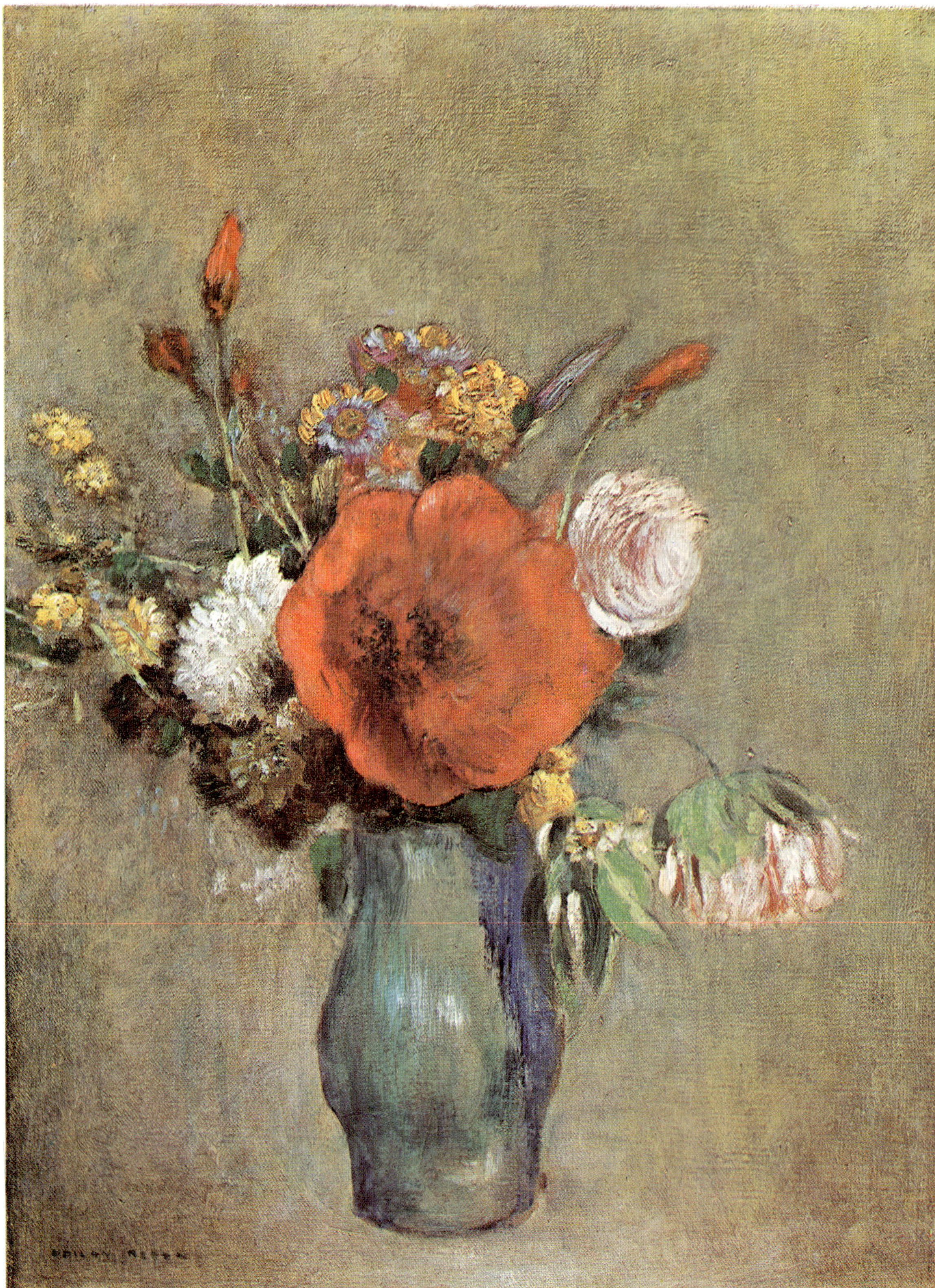

39. *Vase with Flowers and Butterflies* -
Private collection, USA.

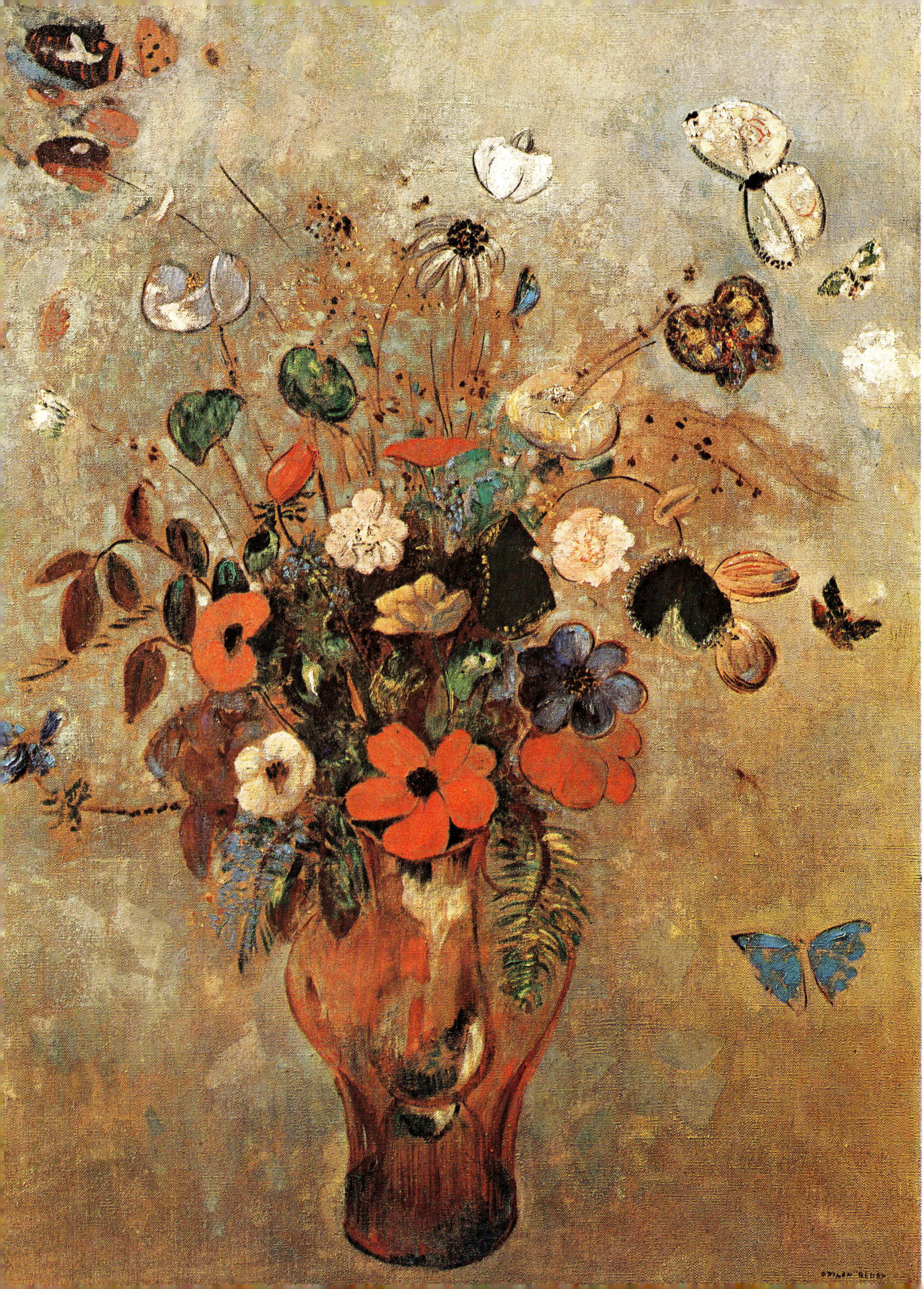

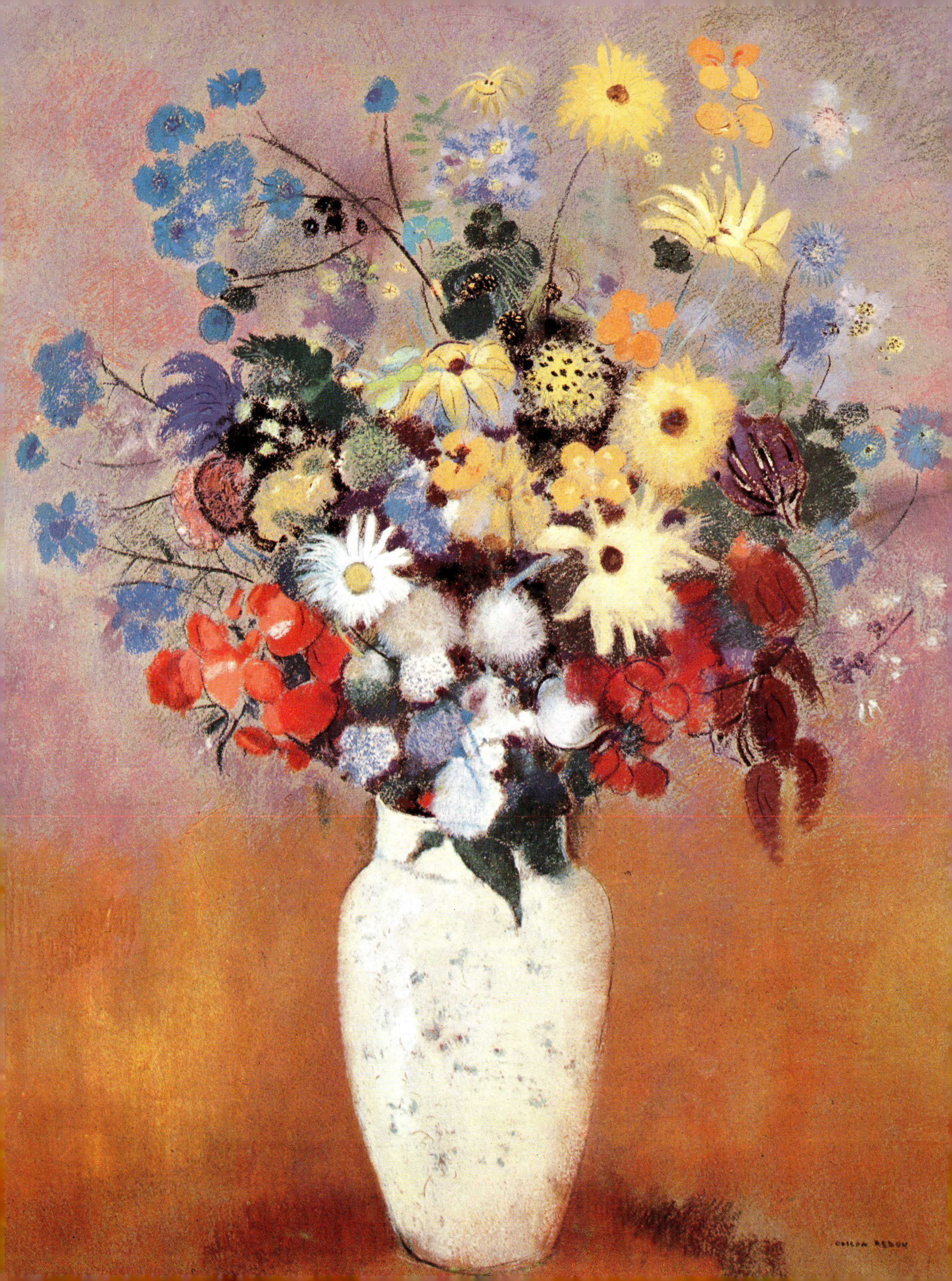

40. *Vase of Flowers* - 1912 ca. Musée du Louvre, Paris.

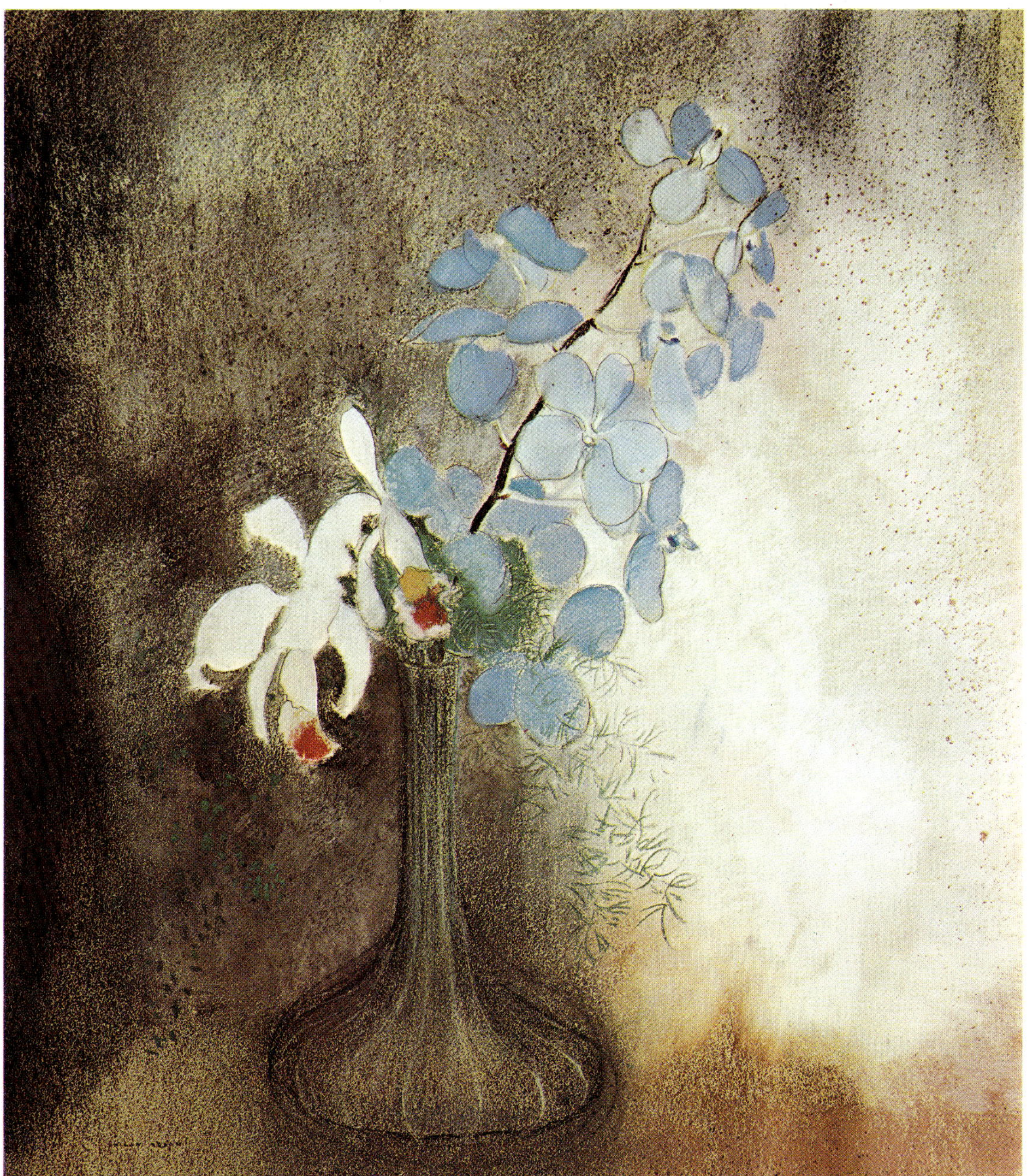

41. *Orchid* - 1912 ca. Private collection, USA.

42. *Shell* - 1912. Private collection, Paris.

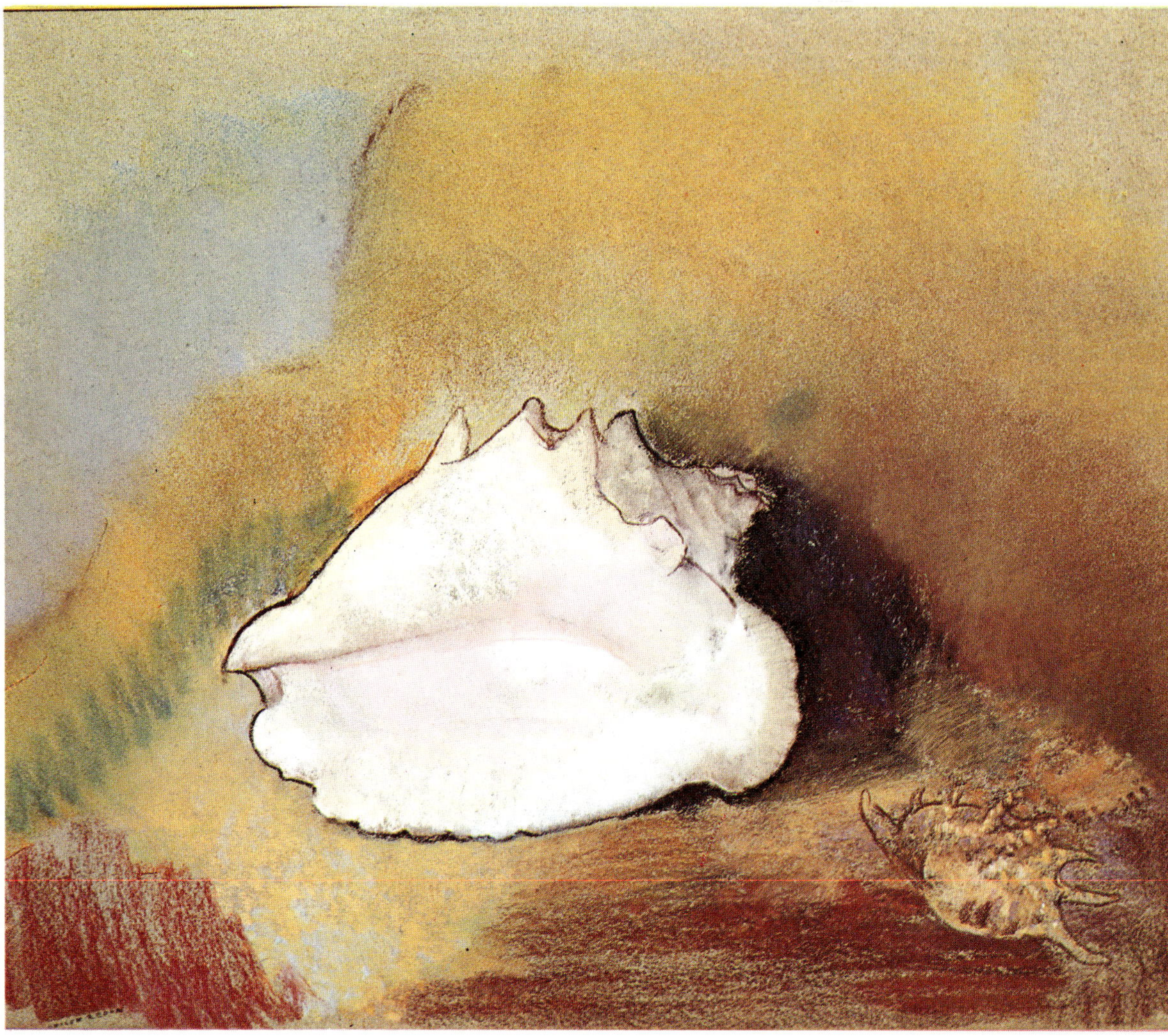

43. *Butterflies* - 1910 ca. Private collection, USA.

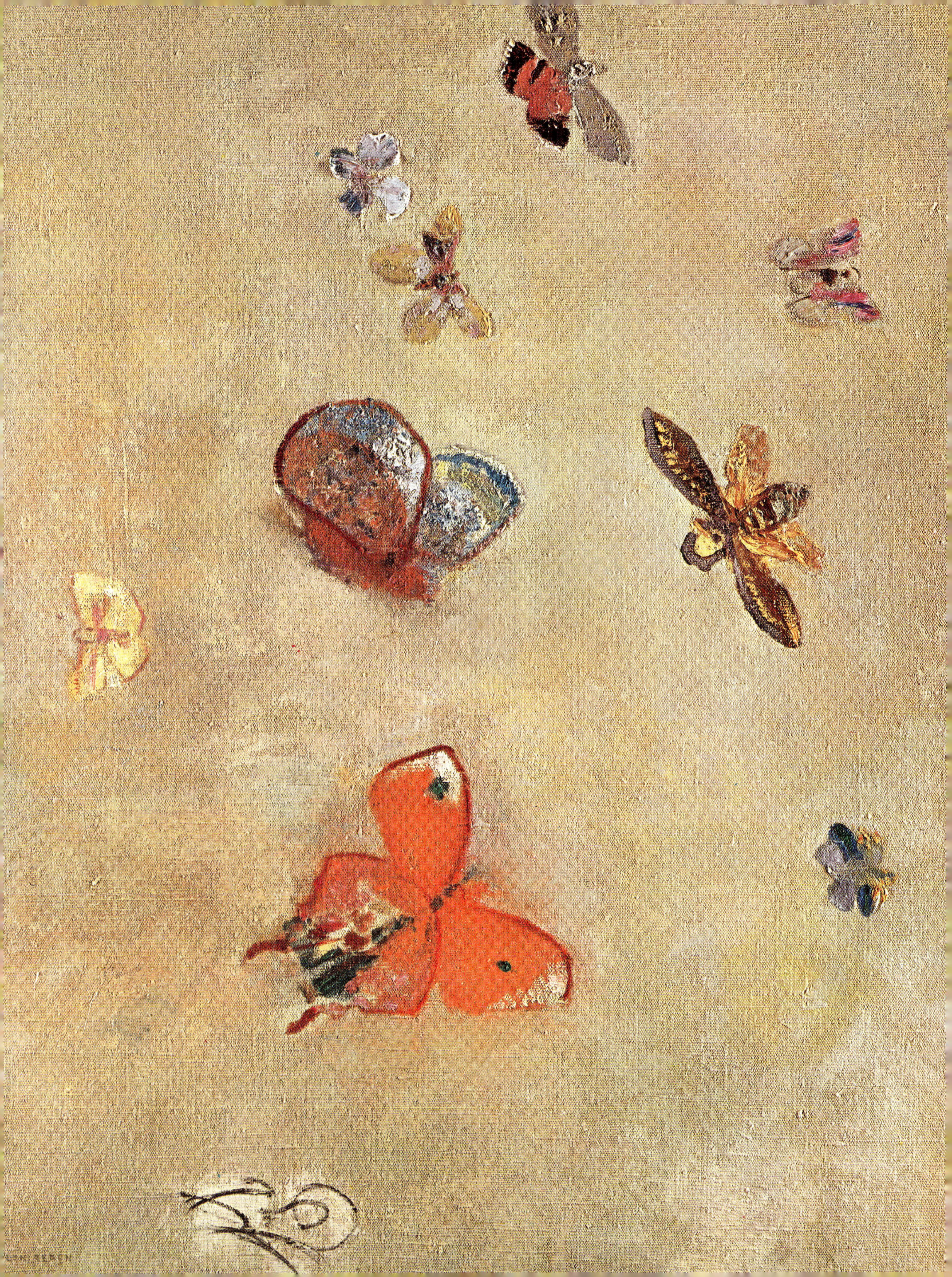

44. *The Red Tree* - 1906. Private collection.

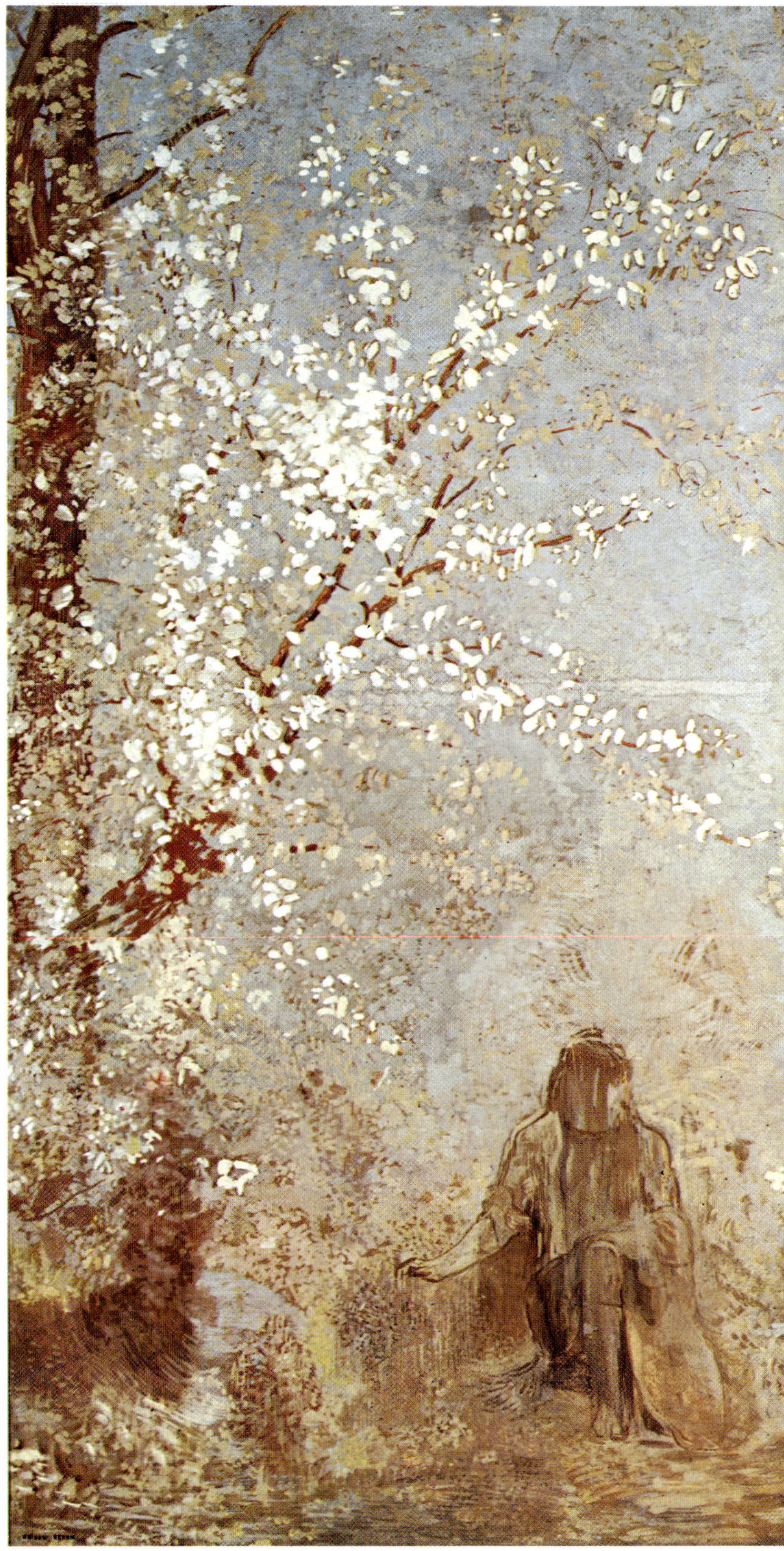

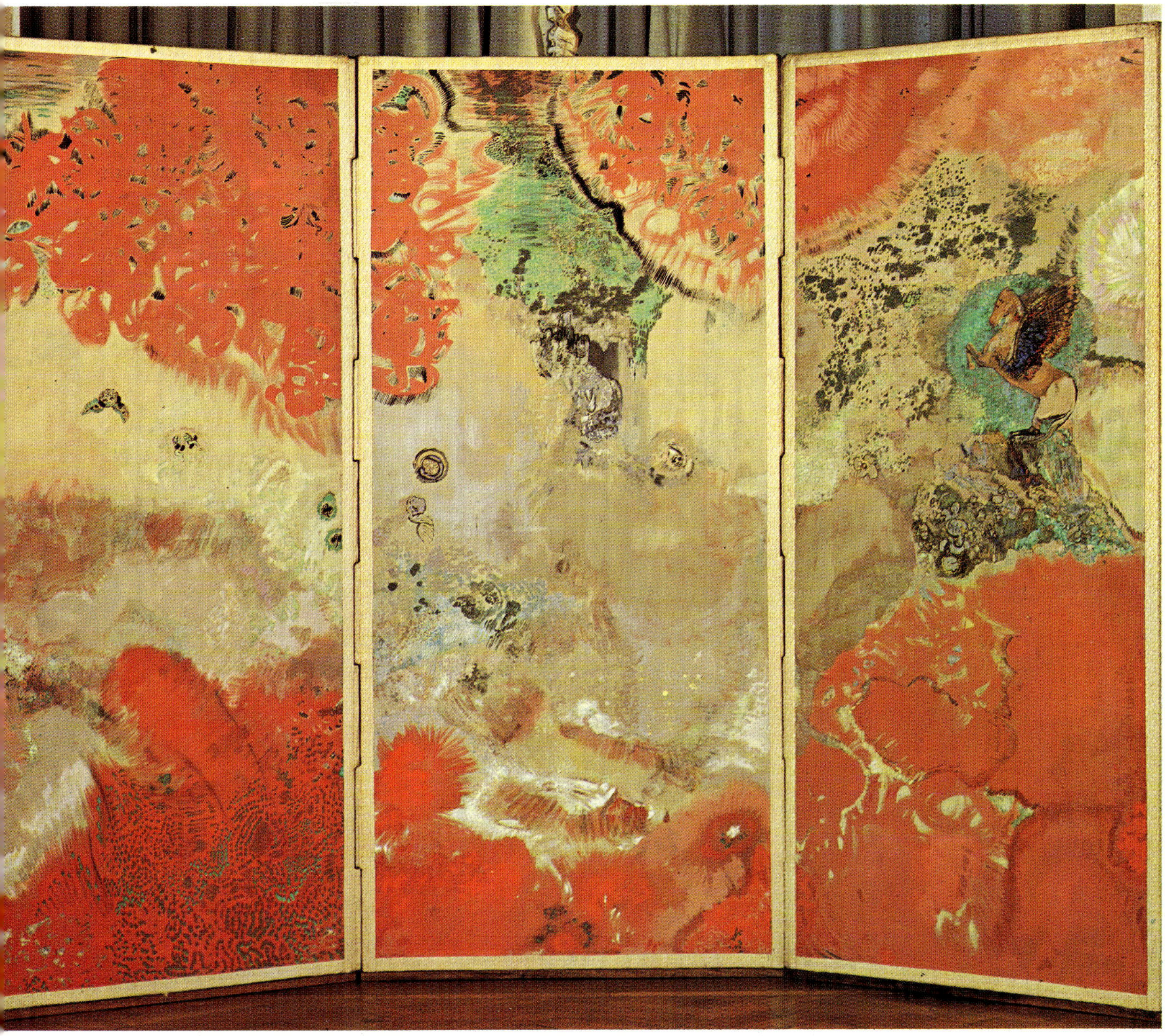

45. *The Red Screen* - 1906-1908. Private collection

Editor in chief Anna Maria Mascheroni

Art director Luciano Raimondi

Text Edda Fonda

Translation Terrence Rogers

Production DIMA & B, Milan

Photo Credits Gruppo Editoriale Fabbri S.p.A., Milan

ISBN 2-89393-048-4

Printed in Italy by Gruppo Editoriale Fabbri S.p.A., Milan